NUMBER TWENTY-SEVEN:
The Walter Prescott Webb Memorial Lectures

Essays on
English Law and the American Experience

[THE WALTER PRESCOTT WEBB MEMORIAL LECTURES]

Essays on English Law and the American Experience

BY WILLIAM R. JONES, CRAIG EVAN KLAFTER,
THOMAS P. SLAUGHTER, ELISABETH A. CAWTHON,
YASUHIDE KAWASHIMA, AND CALVIN WOODARD

Introduction by Richard Hamm
Edited by Elisabeth A. Cawthon
and David E. Narrett

Published for the University of Texas at Arlington by
Texas A&M University Press: College Station

First edition

The paper used in this book meets the minimum requirements of the American National Standard for Permanence of Paper for Printed Library Materials, Z39.48–1984.
Binding materials have been chosen for durability.
∞

Library of Congress Cataloging-in-Publication Data

Essays on English law and the American experience / by William R. Jones . . . [et al.] ; edited by Elisabeth A. Cawthon and David E. Narrett ; introduction by Richard Hamm.
p. cm.—(The Walter Prescott Webb memorial lectures, 27)
ISBN 0-89096-581-1 (alk. paper)
1. Common law—United States. 2. Law—United States—History. 3. Law—Great Britain—History. I. Jones, William R., 1930– II. Cawthon, Elisabeth A., 1957– . III. Narrett, David E., 1951– . IV. Series.
KF394.A2E87 1994
349.42—dc20
[344.2]
93-34549
CIP

To Jenkins Garrett

Contents

Preface

The twenty-seventh annual Walter Prescott Webb Memorial Lectures had as their focus the influence of English law in the late eighteenth- and nineteenth-century United States. On the campus of the University of Texas at Arlington, on March 12, 1992, participants in the Webb lecture series considered the doctrinal heritage of English law and its considerable modifications by Americans who both cherished the Anglo-American legal heritage and were determined to alter it to suit particular political, social, and economic circumstances. The present volume contains the results of the research of the lecturers, as well as the writings of the winners of the annual Webb-Smith essay competition. The writers, informed by their understanding of Anglo-American law and history, make a case not only for the influence of English law and legal thought in American history, but for the vitality of comparative legal history as a discipline.

The contributors to this volume are scholars with a broad range of interests and experience in the study and teaching of legal history. Each has an academic background in both United States and English history, as well as other areas of comparative history and law. The author of the introduction, Richard Hamm, is assistant professor of history and public policy at the University of Albany, State University of New York. He also has served as a teaching fellow at Princeton University. An expert in nineteenth-century U.S. constitutional history, Professor Hamm has written *Shaping the Eighteenth Amendment: Temperance Reform, Legal Culture, and the Polity, 1880–1920,* which is a forthcoming publication in the University of North Carolina's legal history series. His articles on southern legal history and the history of taxation have appeared in several historical journals.

William Jones, professor of history at the University of New Hampshire, is the author of "Relations of the Two Jurisdictions: Conflict and Cooperation of the Royal and Ecclesiastical Courts in England during the Thirteenth and Fourteenth Centuries," in *Studies in Medieval and*

Renaissance History. He has written numerous articles on comparative law in the medieval and early modern periods. As an active participant in international scholarly conferences, he has lectured on topics from slander to royal fund-raising to the legal status of religious minorities. Professor Jones, a former chair of the department of history at the University of New Hampshire, has received several awards in recognition of outstanding undergraduate teaching and legal studies advising.

Craig Evan Klafter, a co-winner of the Webb-Smith essay competition, received advanced degrees from the University of Chicago and Oxford University. A respected scholar of Anglo-American history in the American Revolutionary period and the history of the legal profession, he divides his time between research in the United States and his duties as research fellow in legal history at the University of Southampton. His book, *Reason Over Precedents: Origins of American Legal Thought,* is a forthcoming publication of Greenwood Press.

Thomas P. Slaughter is an authority on the political history of the early republic. He is the author of books including *Bloody Dawn: The Christiana Riot and Racial Violence in the Antebellum North* and *The Whiskey Rebellion: Frontier Epilogue to the American Revolution,* which was a History Book Club selection. A professor of history at Rutgers University, he has served as well as director of the graduate program in history. Dr. Slaughter, a graduate of the University of Maryland and Princeton University, has been an important contributor to debates among scholars of English history and U.S. history, in publications such as the *New York Review of Books.*

Elisabeth A. Cawthon is assistant professor of history at the University of Texas at Arlington. Her research centers on Anglo-American law and labor history, and the intersections between legal history and medical history. Among her publications are "New Life for the Deodand, Occupational Accidents and the Law," in the *American Journal of Legal History.* With Steven Reinhardt, Professor Cawthon co-edited volume twenty-five in the Webb Lectures series, *Essays on the French Revolution: Paris and the Provinces.*

Yasuhide Kawashima, an authority on law and native Americans in the southwestern United States, is the author of *Puritan Justice and the Indian: White Man's Law in Massachusetts, 1630–1763* and has edited the New England volumes of *Early American Indian Documents: Treaties and Laws, 1607–1789.* His research on southwestern and Indian history, and environmental regulation, has appeared in several journals and the *Encyclopedia of Historic American Court Cases.* A co-winner of the Webb Smith essay competition, Dr. Kawashima is professor of history at the University of Texas at El Paso.

Calvin Woodard is Henry L. and Grace Doherty professor of law at the school of law of the University of Virginia. Professor Woodard has served as a visiting professor at Stanford University, Washington and Lee Law School, and National Chengchi University, Taiwan. A renowned instructor of law students, undergraduates, and sitting judges, Professor Woodard has written on a wide variety of topics in legal philosophy and modern legal history, including his introduction to the Legal Classics Library new edition of von Ghering's *The Struggle for Law.* His pathbreaking reviews in the *New York Times Book Review* include commentaries on the writings of Lawrence Friedman, Roberto Unger, and Richard Posner.

David E. Narrett, co-editor of this volume, is associate professor of history at the University of Texas at Arlington. Dr. Narrett's book, *Inheritance and Family Life in Colonial New York City,* a recent publication of Cornell University Press, received the 1992 Hendricks Manuscript Award for the best historical study on the Dutch colonial experience in North America. Dr. Narrett co-edited, with Joyce Goldberg, volume twenty-two in the Webb Lectures Series, *Essays on Liberty and Federalism: The Shaping of the U.S. Constitution.*

On behalf of the UTA history department, the editors would like to acknowledge several benefactors of the Webb lectures. C. B. Smith, Sr., an Austin businessman and former student of Walter Prescott Webb, generously established the Webb Endowment Fund and made possible the publication of the lectures. Jenkins and Virginia Garrett of Fort Worth have long shown both loyalty and generosity to UTA. At this year's lectures, Mr. Garrett served as an introducer for his fellow attorney, Professor Calvin Woodard. Recently the Webb lecture series has received major support from the Rudolf Hermanns' Endowment for the Liberal Arts, with the encouragement of both longtime UTA president Wendall Nedderman and UTA's new president, Ryan Amacher.

We also would like to acknowledge the assistance of Kenneth Philp, chairman of the history department, and the dedication of Stephen Maizlish, head of the Webb lectures committee. For their expert advice on technical matters, the editors are grateful to Professors Laverne Prewitt,

Stanley Palmer, and Charles Zelden. History graduate students and members of Phi Alpha Theta provided efficient and cordial support during the week of the lectures. A productive and unusual aspect of the twenty-seventh annual lectures was the participation of several jurists, including Judges William Arnot, Joseph Del Sole, Robert Gammage, Donnie Burgess, and Joe C. Spurlock II. The conviviality of the scholarly discussions heard at these lectures was a result of the eagerness of students and members of the university and local community to discuss legal history, and the charm and intellectual generosity of the visiting scholars. The editors are grateful to have been a part of that discourse.

Elisabeth A. Cawthon
David E. Narrett

Essays on
English Law and the American Experience

RICHARD HAMM

Introduction: English Law and the American Experience

In Harper Lee's *To Kill a Mockingbird* there is a small incident that speaks to the theme of this volume. The children of lawyer Atticus Finch go to church with their black housekeeper, Calpurnia. At her church the congregation sings its hymns by "linin": having one of the literate members of the congregation read each line of the hymn before it is sung. Calpurnia's son, Zeebo, reads the verses this day. His literacy prompts Jem and Scout to ask Calpurnia how he learned to read. She answers that she had taught him out of the Bible and a book that their Granddaddy Finch had given her: Blackstone's *Commentaries*. "Jem was thunderstruck. 'You mean you taught Zeebo outa *that?*' 'Why yes sir, Mister Jem. . . . They were the only books I had. Your grandaddy said Mr. Blackstone wrote fine English.'"[1] That Blackstone's *Commentaries* could reach African Americans living in segregated Alabama, and that it could stand shoulder to shoulder with the Bible, shows the pervasiveness of English legal traditions in the United States. The six essays gathered here explore some of the complexities of the deep penetration of English law into the American legal system.

In examining the effect of English law on American law these essays necessarily examine one of the most fruitful areas of legal history scholarship: the nexus between social forces and the relatively autonomous legal system. While it is almost axiomatic that society shapes law, it should not be assumed that law is merely reflexive. Rather, the details of society (social values, political culture, and ideology) interact with the ideas and structures of law to shape legal forms, habits, and processes. That the authors in this volume have the common focus of seeking British origins of American law and life brings into focus the autonomous characteristics of law. In the American context, English doctrine and practice were alien and self-contained; they were separated by the Atlantic Ocean from their social roots. These essayists' examinations of the notion of sanctuary, the development of fencing law on the great plains, the shaping of the American law of treason, the British origins of the Texas workers' compensation system, the Americanization of Blackstone by St. George Tucker, and the exploration of the meaning of common law in the United States all contribute to our greater understanding of how society shapes law.[2]

The relationships between society and law are not merely academic topics. As Calvin Woodard points out, given the turmoil in eastern Europe and the Far East, the likelihood of fundamental legal reorganization is high. As the West tries to remake the economies and political systems elsewhere, so too is the West influencing legal systems in the rest of the world. Woodard's "Is the United States a Common Law Country?" examines the common law tradition in both England and America. His essay is an attempt to determine the legal values that can be attributed to the common law, which "we should most wish to share." Central to his understanding of the common law, the very center of English law, is the paradoxical notion of the autonomy of common law from authority, while it asserts its own authority. The common law system, Woodard argues, creates an attitude that begins "with a question ('what is the law?') not with an answer ('The law is . . .')." It forces people to think about law, not merely follow it—to ask how society should use law.

Common law is of course the "unwritten law" made not by legislatures, but by courts, lawyers, and judges in cases. The source of common law is presumed to be custom, reason, or natural law. In England, the system had its creation when kings issued charters acknowledging the authority of "ancient customs" and created royal courts. These courts and the lawyers who practiced there interpreted the ancient customs, metamorphosing them into common law. Woodard points out that for eight-hundred years the common law was a truly unwritten law controlled by the guildlike Inns of Court, from whom all judges and practicers in the courts came. The Inns existed as autonomous institutions, and shared exclusive knowledge of the opinions of the judges on cases. The judges' opinions given orally were scrutinized by the members of the Inns and used to illuminate the ancient customs; the judges became oracles of the law. Thus lawyers' interpretations of judges' opinions became the principles of common law. It was an intricate system that was closed to all but members of the fraternity. But by the eighteenth century the Inns' symbiotic relations with the courts had collapsed.

Yet the important foundation was laid; the common law had been created. It was a law not rooted in the code of an authority but in ancient customs and general principles. Among its ideas was the notion that the common law was superior to earthly, even royal, authority. Indeed, in the seventeenth century the lawyers' law conflicted with assertions of power by the king. Some lawyers and judges sided with the law rather than the king, and they chose the winning side. When the king lost his struggle for supremacy, common law gained an antiauthoritarian cast. Of course this tendency sat uneasily with the new rulers, who set about trying to limit the common law. The doctrine of "parliamentary sovereignty" allowed rulers to bypass inconvenient common law rules. And it was the application of parliamentary supremacy that began the American revolution.

While the views of common law among revolutionary-era Americans remain ambiguous, it is undeniable that the American retreat from the common law system began around the time of Independence. On one hand, Americans recognized and revered common law for its ideas of natural justice, rule of law, and liberty; on the other they rejected its "Englishness" and vexatious vagaries.[3] The revolutionary generation, by adopting written state and national constitutions, rejected the foundation of common law. The constitutions were written and derived their powers from the sovereign people rather than from ancient English custom. Moreover, they specified how law was to be made and which authorities could make law. Those authorities soon made law at a tremendous rate; by the early nineteenth century, American states and the Federal government began issuing full codes of law. The retreat from the common law continued; there was no autonomous legal institution that compared to the Inns of Court in the new nation, to assure that lawyers fully learned the common law and to police their application of what they did know. Eventually new ideas about law pushed the old ones from the American lawyers' minds. From the Civil War to the present, new concepts of law—many of them borrowed from the civil law tradition—reshaped American law. Thus legal science, sociological jurisprudence, the jurisprudence of interests, administrative law, criminology, and legal realism all replaced common law. This declension of the common law was not only an American phenomenon.

In the course of the nineteenth and twentieth centuries, England effectively abandoned common law. Convinced by reformers and the changes in economy and society that the common law failed to meet the needs of the age, Parliament through statutes changed the content of the law. In the courts, the idea of *stare decisis* became an ironclad rule—all the more confining because the previous rulings were no longer the exclusive knowledge of lawyers. In the 1870s the newly established Supreme Court of Judicature was placed atop the court system, and its published opinions became easily accessible. In the twentieth century, England created a welfare state governed through administrative law. The substance and procedures of twentieth-century English law differ drastically from the common law. But, ironically, Woodard notes that key notions of common law survived in the American federal judiciary, even after England's modern abandonment of common law.

The American judiciary by the nineteenth century, and persisting to today, have become the oracles of the law. In their interpretations of the Constitution and their application of judicial review of legislation and administrative law, the justices have reinvented the common law wheel. The judges assume the power to nullify legislation and regulation they deem "unconstitutional." Theirs is an assertion of higher law, and often is as mysterious to the uninitiated as the ancient customs of a previous age. Significantly, the idea of law, not authority, is celebrated in judicial review. Every case brought to challenge a law or rule asks the question, "What is the law?" Ultimately, then, the common law tradition is an idea that prompts more questions, such as "Why this law?" and "What is the purpose of law?" Woodard's argument that such ancient ideas can have modern consequences is a point illustrated in the contribution of William Jones.

Jones's "Sanctuary, Exile, and the Law: The Fugitive and Public Authority in Medieval England and Modern America" looks at the deep historical roots of a recent phenomenon: the sanctuary movement. Jones examines legal institutions that almost disappeared in England before the colonization of America. Indeed, Jones maintains that the modern sanctuary movement does not derive from the English tradition. In showing that discontinuity, Jones sketches out a complicated history of sanctuary and related ideas of exile, abjuration, and outlawry in England. He argues that the rise and fall of sanctuary in England intersected with the changing nature of society and the state from the seventh century to the sixteenth.

In its near-millennium of existence, sanctuary always stood at the boundary between state and church. Despite analogues in ancient religious traditions, sanctuary emerged in Europe with the rise of Christianity; the church as a holy place was central to the formation and workings of sanctuary. Civil authorities accepted and indeed fostered the system. In Anglo-Saxon England, sanctuary occurred in a polity governed by customary and communal law. The law rested on self-help, arbitration, and compensation; and behind it always lay the possibility of blood feud, which threatened to disrupt the community. The Saxon kings supported the sanctuary system through laws that married the kingdom to the system. Their laws facilitated the settlement of felonious disputes by defining who could seek sanctuary, what churches could grant it, and what fines (to the king) and compensations (to individuals) must be paid. In doing so, they made sanctuary part of the public law.

In post-Conquest England, the new rulers built on this foundation. In particular, they added the idea of abjuration—voluntary exile from the realm—to sanctuary. Thus in the later medieval period, when the system flourished, a criminal sought sanctuary in church, confessed to crime in public before royal officials, and adjured the realm. Theoretically, the criminal was then escorted by royal officials to the port for exile. The sanctuary system was now integrated into the new political culture, which replaced communal law aimed at arbitrating disputes with a public authority concerned with restraining crime. But like much of the medieval state, sanctuary failed to live up to expectations. During much of the medieval period, probably few abjurors ever left the kingdom; instead the system worked as a public notification network, naming the crime and criminal, and legally barring the criminal from the community. As the centuries passed, the crown sought to curb sanctuary abuses and limit its reach. Abjuration was enforced and various criminal acts were excluded from sanctuary.

By the sixteenth and seventeenth centuries, however, the principles of sanctuary disappeared, and the state limited the practice. The English reformation took away sanctuary's religious basis by making the church a national church. Sanctuary came to be viewed as a hindrance to the king's authority to administer justice. Acting on these premises, Tudor and Stuart leaders curtailed and eventually destroyed sanctuary, first subjecting the privilege to stringent limitations as to what kinds of felons were admitted to sanctuary. More sweepingly, Henry VIII's Parliament stripped abjuration from the process of sanctuary, forcing those who sought it to become prisoners for life in the church. In 1624 the final step was taken; sanctuary was abolished.

The reemergence of the term in the past thirty years is a strange echo, for by the twentieth century sanctuary was long dead in English law and practice. But sanctuary had dramatic attraction for Americans unhappy with the actions of their state. Protestors of the Vietnam war and opponents of the Reagan and Bush Administrations' Central American policies (particularly, it should be noted, Catholic activists) tried to revive the idea of sanctuary. They created organizations dedicated to shielding draft objectors and foreign refugees (classified as illegal aliens) from the government. Given the realities of the modern state, which engrosses all law unto itself and permits no alternatives, it is unlikely that these groups' attempts to carve out their own enclaves from state power are anything more than symbolic. The sanctuary movements are designed primarily to draw attention to government policy to prompt its changes. Like medieval English sanctuary, they exist within the confines of social and governing arrangements. Similarly, fences—and the laws that support them—are creations of lawmakers' view of society.

Yasuhide Kawashima's, "Fence Laws on the Great Plains, 1865–1900," explores the changing fence law patterns and practices of eight American plains states. Kawashima shows that in the period from the ending of the Civil War to the closing of the frontier, the fence law of these states underwent a similar evolution, from a policy of "fencing out," which required farmers to protect their crops, to "fencing in," which required stock owners to restrain their animals. These changes in fencing law reflected transformations in society, especially changing use of the land and the emergence of new means to build fences. This pattern of alteration ended with the states of the great plains adopting a policy that returned them to the position of the English common law. Kawashima's essay can be said to detail the "rediscovery" of the British roots of American law.

The English common law policy of "fencing in" was one of two traditions that the creators of fence laws on the great plains inherited. Common law made owners of animals strictly liable for their animals. When their animals caused harm on others' land, the owner of the beasts paid. Thus the law imposed a duty on owners to keep their animals off others' land. But in Britain's American colonies, and in the new nation, the English rule was abandoned; the colonies required landowners to fence out trespassing domestic animals. If farmers did not make good fences, they could not recover for damages incurred from wandering beasts. In the southeast, landholders were prohibited from fencing uncultivated land, thus promoting an open range where anyone could let their animals graze. In the northeast, the fencing out pattern persisted through the eighteenth century even as the land became heavily settled; the preservation of commons for grazing seemed to validate the practice of letting animals wander. In the less heavily settled south, the practice of open range persisted with little opposition through Reconstruction.

While lawmakers on the great plains were aware of the English common law rule, their initial policy preference was to join the American rejection of it by writing laws requiring the fencing of crops. In jurisdiction after jursidiction, upon the initial settlement, legislatures created laws requiring cultivators to "sufficiently" fence in their crops. The courts enforced both the letter and spirit of these laws, holding that insufficient fences constituted negligence and barred recovery. One state supreme court held that the very presence of the state's statute superseded the common law tradition. The statute law protected the grazier, even limiting farmers' right to defend against animals wandering onto their lands. This was a hard burden for farmers, for much of the land of the great plains lacked available timber to construct fences. Even after the invention of barbed wire, the process of building a fence was costly and time-consuming. At least until the twentieth century, the federal government—greatest landholder in the West—supported the open range. But the cattle drovers and stock raisers did not have the law all their way. "Willful and wanton trespass"—such as deliberately driving stock across any fence, even an inadequate one—gave farmers the right to recover.

In the plains states, over time and through incremental steps, the farmers gained more favorable laws—culminating in statewide policies of fencing in animals. The older plains states like Nebraska and Kansas began the process by enacting night herd laws, requiring the confinement of livestock at night. Typically these laws applied only to certain districts. States across the plains soon began adopting local option laws limiting the open range. These laws allowed voters in a community to suspend the effect of the state fence law. Indeed, at least one court considered that these new laws restored the English common law rule. The local option system seemed to satisfy farmers' needs because it persisted until the twentieth century, when in the first two decades, the states adopted statewide fence policies. The federal government joined in the attack on the open range. The innovation of barbed wire led many grazers to abandon the open range in favor of fenced pastures. Some, in their enthusiasm for the new system, illegally fenced government land for their own exclusive use. This abuse prompted government to restrict grazing on federal land to licensed users—thus ending the free range.

This progression of fence law on the great plains reflected the changing of the nature of society on the plains, from frontier to settled regions. It underscores the instrumental function of the law, for the settlers of the great plains clearly wanted a law that would foster their economy and way of life. As grazing was replaced by farming as the staple of the economy, the fence out gave way to the fence in. In this striking interplay of law and society, English law—the old common law rule of strict liability for animal owners—served as a model for those unhappy with the free range. The notion of the English law as model was an idea at the forefront of how lawmakers perceived one of the classic works of law: Blackstone's *Commentaries.*

Craig E. Klafter's "The Americanization of Blackstone's *Commentaries*" explores how Americans, after the revolution, adopted Blackstone. He shows that although Blackstone was immensely popular in the United States, and especially important in educating lawyers, Americans did not accept the work unalloyed. Rather, mostly through the efforts of the Jeffersonian Republican theorist St. George Tucker, Americans adopted a version of the *Commentaries* that reflected their (or at least Tucker's) political ideology and social values. Blackstone's *Commentaries* became the foundation for American lawyers to help build a republican polity and egalitarian social structure.

Of course, such a social and political structure was alien to William Blackstone. He intended his *Commentaries,* four volumes long and first published in 1765, to teach the English elite—the landed classes—how to use the law to safeguard their social and political positions. He did so by "naturalizing" the common law—that is, conflating it (in all its unsystematic detail) with natural law. He used the oppressive details of the common law to demonstrate the fundamental principles of law. According to Blackstone, these principles were immutable and natural—beyond human reason. The key principle illustrated by Blackstone's work is the supremacy, in law, of the right to property. The complexity of the tenure system, which limited the alienation and distribution of real estate and limited suffrage based on landholding, became, not creatures of human creation, but manifestations of natural law. Through his systematizing, and through his clarity of style, Blackstone made both the detail and principles of law easily comprehensible.

American lawyers found Blackstone's *Commentaries* appealing. It filled an important gap in the legal literature: that of primer for aspiring lawyers. Nowhere else could a student gain so much knowledge of the common law. After the revolution and in the early nineteenth century there was a tremendous demand for more lawyers; thus, legal educators used Blackstone, despite his antirepublican agenda. For some conservative Federalists, Blackstone's values made his work even more attractive. The majority of the bar, however, worried about his biases and feared entrenching in the minds of lawyers, and thus in the law, Blackstone's precepts. They feared the corrosive effects of his social and political vision on republican institutions. Until Chancellor James Kent brought out his *Commentaries on American Law* in 1826, Blackstone was the key text. But it was a version of Blackstone made safe for American institutions by St. George Tucker that saw so much use.

In reworking Blackstone, Tucker drew upon a counter-tradition concerning the nature of law. This tradition was encapsulated in Montesquieu's *The Spirit of the Laws,* a work popular in both the colonies and new nation. While Montesquieu believed in inalienable rights and the laws of nature, he also embraced relativism. In his philosophical treatment of law, Montesquieu maintained that law reflected the "general spirit" of a nation as created by its climate, religion, economy, morality, and customs. Nature required that laws apply to a given society; lawmakers should only make laws to fit a given society. Reason became the tool to determine the soundness of a law for a nation. Thus Montesquieu, and other European philosophers, gave Tucker the means to temper the "anti-American" elements of Blackstone's *Commentaries*—by pointing out where Blackstone's ideas did not suit American society.

In the 1790s, Tucker began his recasting of Blackstone through his teaching, and was soon at work on an annotated version of the *Commentaries.* It was published in 1803 and remained the standard American edition until 1852. In his notes and appendix, Tucker pointed out junctures at which Blackstone's exposition of English law was unsuitable to the United States. Politically, of course, Blackstone was a poor fit. His espousal of parliamentary supremacy and his denial to colonists the liberties of the common law violated the foundations of the republic: inalienable rights found in the common law and the sovereignty of the people. Beyond politics, Tucker argued that the American experience altered the law, making parts of Blackstone's explanation of private law inappropriate for the new nation. Tucker pointed out that the the colonies and early states already had changed many aspects of the law to fit their situation. In particular, Tucker argued for rejection of Blackstone's view of the law of property. Tucker substituted a system that promoted easy acquisition and free alienation of land for the restrictive, aristocratically biased system of English common law.

Tucker's edition undermined the central core of Blackstone's work. It replaced revelation and immutable principles with relativism and reason. It rejected the social and political assumptions of the author. It made the *Commentaries* "safe" for a republican and enterprising nation. Tucker's political ideology transformed English law into American law, without changing the title. While others have argued that Blackstone's influence was "unfettered," Klafter shows that there was more going on than mindless borrowing. A similar pattern emerges in the creation of the American law of treason.

Thomas P. Slaughter's "The Politics of Treason in the 1790s" examines the development of treason law in the early republic. He points out that indigenous developments, not mere borrowing from England, shaped the development of a restricted American law of treason. While the founders—mostly notably James Wilson—borrowed heavily from England in writing the Constitution's treason clause, the political culture of the revolution and struggles of the 1790s actually laid the foundation of the American conception and practice. His essay underscores the collective point of this work—that social forces, in this case political ideology and power, shape law, but that they build law out of the available material, such as English treason law.

Anglo-American treason law originated in the actions of medieval Englishmen who sought to safeguard a state based on kingship. The bedrock of treason was the statute known as 25 Edward III, which delineated a list of offenses that constituted treason. It included three areas that saw much doctrinal development: compassing or imagining the king's death, levying war against the king, and adhering to the king's enemies. The penalties for treason included a terrible death and "corruption of the blood"—penalties inflicted on the families of traitors. The fourteenth and fifteenth centuries saw an expansion of treasonable offenses, adding all sorts of crimes to treason. At the same time, a procedural protection for accused emerged: a confession or two witnesses were usually necessary to prove treason. But in the sixteenth century these protections disappeared in the prerogative courts of the Tudors.

In the seventeenth century, Stuart judges, while ignoring procedural safeguards in treason trials, embarked on a course of judicial construction of new treasons. The judges expanded the ideas of compassing or imagining the king's death and levying war to mammoth proportions, resulting in some of the most notorious judicial barbarity in English history. In the wake of the Glorious Revolution, Parliament restored procedural protections in treason trials, including the "two witness rule"; but it did nothing to check the potential of constructive treasons; moreover the procedural protections were ignored in practice. James Wilson in writing the Constitution's section on treason drew not upon this chaotic heritage directly but rather a more orderly view of English treason law created by commentators.

Misreading the English experience through the works of the common law commentators—Hale, Coke, Foster, and Blackstone—was only one element that went into the writing of the constitution's treason clause. Wilson and other Americans reading the commentators believed their account that the English law of treason was evolving to a fairer law, which protected the rights of Englishmen. They sought to apply those protections and more to their own nation. American political culture changed the basic rules of the polity. Given the republican nature of the revolution, protections for the king's life disappeared from the definition of treason, thereby removing one of the most judicially expanded areas of treason law from the American experience.

But much remained. Wilson borrowed almost verbatim the passage on treason from English law, only changing terms to make them fit the republican realities. The section defines treason as consisting of "only in levying war against" the United States "or in adhering to their enemies, giving them aid and comfort. No person shall be convicted of treason unless on the testimony of two witnesses to the same overt act, or on confession in open court." It gave congress "Power to declare the Punishment of Treason, but no Attainder of Treason shall work Corruption of Blood, or Forfeiture except during the Life of the Person attainted." Wilson thought that he had built upon a liberal English foundation by constitutionalizing the definition and safeguards, removing from the legislature the power to make new treasons, stipulating a modicum of safeguards, and limiting the punishments. But the section allowed, by implication, judicial construction of treason. Federalist judges did not hesitate to use their power to interpret treason law.

During a decade of fierce political struggle in the 1790s, the Federalist party, in control of the federal government, engaged in a variety of campaigns to crush political and popular opposition to its policies. One of its means was bringing treason charges against various citizens who had engaged in resistance to federal taxes. As the Sedition Act and the hysterical denunciation of the Jeffersonian Republicans revealed, the Federalists did not understand the concept of a loyal opposition; to them all political opposition verged on treason. Federalist Judges Patterson, Peterson, and Chase, in various trials, created broad constructive treasons of levying war, stretched the two witness requirement beyond credibility, and adopted a view of an "overt act" that included things that were anything but overt or an act. Yet politics, which demanded a strong treason law, also demanded mercy. Washington and later Adams pardoned the convicted in each successful treason case. But the political reality changed.

After 1800, the Federalist judges found themselves political outcasts in a government dominated by Jeffersonian Republicans. Their new situation coincided with their revitalization of the procedural protections and questioning of constructive treasons. The Jeffersonians were no more accepting of the idea of legitimate opposition than the Federalists had been. They began impeachment proceedings against Judge Chase, one of the most intemperate of Federalist judges. It was revealing—at least on the issue of treason law—that the bills of impeachment did not fault Chase for his constructive treason. While the impeachment failed, Federalist judges fought back by shaping the law to a new reality. John Marshall, for instance, in presiding over Aaron Burr's treason trial, revitalized the two witnesses rule.

For various reasons, including that they were difficult to win, treason prosecutions declined in popularity. Judges of the nineteenth century—working in an environment that recognized legitimate political strife—returned to the clear meaning of restrictions of the Constitution, taking its words literarily, establishing the limited scope and procedural safeguards that define American treason law. Significantly, this return to a rule of law—to an autonomous of power conception of law—emerged out of political struggle. It illuminates how complicated the nexus of society and law can be. Similarly Elisabeth A. Cawthon's work shows that borrowing from the English tradition—which was autonomous from the American experience—does not mean that the law borrowed was fair.

Cawthon's "Rough Work and Tough Logic: The English Roots of Texas Workers' Compensation Law" explains why the handling of injured workers has been remarkably similar in the legal systems of England and Texas. In the Anglo-American world in the last two centuries, the law of injured workers has moved through four different conceptional periods—though various jurisdictions have adopted a particular view of the matter at different times. She shows that the creation of the changing rules revolved around the assignment of the costs of industrial development, not legal ideology. A changing economy and society prompted changes in legal institutions, conceptions of the law, and the power of the state to act in the interest in the welfare of its citizens. But when the conceptions changed, injured workers seemed to come out the losers.

In the first conceptional period—which existed prior to the 1830s and 1840s—injuries to workers fell under the rubric of "law of master and servant." The dominant doctrine was *respondeat superior:* that is, masters were duty-bound to assist those workers injured on jobs. This idea was rooted in the notion of workers being members of a "family," and represented the reality of the small-scale shops. But the rhetoric was stronger than the reality, for few workers could afford to sue and the best witnesses usually still worked for the employers at fault and were unlikely to testify. While this conception of duties of employers gave the workers little, it was generous compared to the period that followed.

In the 1830s and 1840s, in England and America, judges constructed new doctrines as exceptions to the general rule of *respondeat superior.* England was the birthplace of the first variance from it. Complex interchanges, where doctrine and argument crossed and recrossed the Atlantic, muddied the bloodlines of the various exceptions. These new doctrines, which swallowed the old rule, transformed the law of injury on the job. These rules were the fellow-servant rule, the assumption of risk rule, and contributory negligence doctrine. The fellow-servant rule barred collection of damages from an employer if the injury was caused by the action of a fellow servant. Assumption of risk assumed that the workers when they contracted to take dangerous work negotiated compensation high enough to cover the costs of potential injuries. The doctrine of contributory negligence barred recovery if the employee injured had in any way contributed toward the accident that caused the injury. All these doctrines limited the chances for recovery by injured workers, and thus subsidized industrial development by reducing industrialists' costs.

This bleak picture for injured workers was altered in the third period of workers' injury law. In England and in the American states, reflecting an awareness of the social costs of industrialization, legislatures passed laws prohibiting the application of the restrictive rules. Courts joined in the new reality by redefining some employees. Some supervisors became classified as "vice principals"—that is, employees acting for an employer; if their negligence caused an injury, the injured worker had a right to recovery. In various jurisdictions at this time, thanks to cracks in the legal rules and favorable juries, some workers were winning substantial damage awards for their injuries. This third period in workplace injury law seemed to indicate a maturing industrial economy; it existed between the draconian second period and the current system based on workers' compensation systems.[4]

In the early twentieth century, the English Parliament and American state legislatures constructed workers' compensation plans. Under pressure of reformers and businesses, who felt the sting of jury verdicts, the jurisdictions adopted more rational and predictable compensation systems. These new systems replaced the civil remedies with a compensation scheme sponsored and mandated by the state. Employers either opted to join the plan or were required to join the plan. When workers of a covered firm were injured, the worker could recover only through a set administrative program. The amount of compensation was determined in advance by extensive and complicated tables detailing the compensation for injury, medical expenses, and wages. Fault and liability were unimportant to this system; nor did it allow for punitive damages. Conceptually, workers' compensation replaced employers' liability with concern for the general social costs of workplace injuries. These systems recognized that industrial work was the foundation of the economy and that it was the duty of the state to ameliorate some of its worst effects. The workers' compensation system, despite its unpopularity with many groups, has lasted with minor modifications to the current day. But what explains these "twists and turns in legal rules"? And what explains the timing of these changes?

Cawthon moves beyond existing explanations of the transformations of workplace injury law. She rejects the naive notions of treatise writers who see lawmakers as attempting to put the law in balance so that employees or employers do not experience too much pain. Cawthon also questions the application of Richard Posner's "law and economics" to the shifts in worker safety law. Her work derives from, and moves beyond, the legal historians (Levy, Horwitz, Friedman, Ladinsky, and Tomlins) who have rooted the changes in the law in the shifting economic underpinnings of the Anglo-American world. The Texas example—scattered throughout her essay—adds depth to the explanation of the causes of this legal change.

Changes in Texas workers' injury law reflected transformations of Texas society. Before the 1820s, Spanish and Mexican law was Texas law, putting workplace injury rules in the rubric of contracts. With the influx of Anglo-Americans in the 1820s, the revolt of the 1830s, and the annexation of 1845, common law gained ascendance in Texas. Texas came into the common law world just as the restrictive rules of the second period emerged. But Texas was slow to adopt these rules—its economy, which had few large manufacturing and industrial enterprises, revolved around grazing, farming, and plantation slavery. With the Texas railroad boom of the 1880s, however, when the railroads became major political players in the state, the doctrines of assumption of risk, fellow servant, and contributory negligence came into their own. The law seemed to turn to the new doctrines to promote railroad development in the state.

As the railroads in Texas went from being "engines of growth" into "smoking monsters," the law shifted again. In the 1890s and early twentieth century, politics in the state turned on unsuccessful attempts to tame the railroads, especially the out-of-state lines. As Texas had been late to adopt the second period's conception of workers' injuries, it essentially skipped the third period and jumped in 1910 to the fourth. In that year, the state—under pressure from big business seeking to rationalize its costs—created a workers' compensation system that applied only to industrial workers. Cawthon's account illustrates how the economic and political nature of a society interacted with the English doctrines and examples of other American states to create a system that, with minor tinkering, has lasted until today. The workers' compensation system that exists in Texas—with its lists of payments for missing limbs—echoes the wergelds for personal injury of the oldest of English legal documents, the Anglo-Saxon dooms.

That today's law in Texas reverberates with ideas from old English precepts demonstrates the vitality of the English legal tradition in

America. Just as they carried their plants, the colonists in the seventeenth century carried English legal ideas to the new land. Like the plants of colonists, English law soon jumped the borders of the gardens and rooted itself in the land. Just as dandelion and Kentucky blue grass, common law ideas and practices became a force to reshape the landscape. Even as the invading plants had to adapt to their new environment, however, English law had to respond to the American experience. Often there was agency at work, selecting or rejecting parts of the English law. Still, chance and drift also had their say. The six essays gathered here delineate the forces at work and some of the ways in which the English law has influenced American life. Thus they shed light on the functioning of the law and society nexus.

NOTES

1. Harper Lee, *To Kill a Mockingbird* (New York: Popular Library Edition, 1962), 123–28.

2. A sampling of works that discuss legal autonomy from various perspectives includes E. P. Thompson, *Whigs and Hunters: The Origins of the Black Act* (New York: Pantheon, 1975), esp. 260–69; Lawrence Friedman, *Total Justice* (Boston: Beacon Press, 1985), esp. 38–44, 147–52; Lucy Salyer, "Captives of the Law: Judicial Enforcement of the Chinese Exclusion Laws, 1891–1905," *Journal of American History* 76 (June 1989): 91–117, esp. 116–17; and "Review Symposium: The Work of J. Willard Hurst," *American Bar Foundation Research Journal,* 1985, pp. 113–44.

3. The trend to remake the common law to suit the governing arrangements and social predilections of the ruling classes in England—capped by the publication of Blackstone's *Commentaries*—prompted Americans to announce this allegiance to the seventeenth-century tradition. Hence Thomas Jefferson, as Craig Klafter notes, preferred "my Lord Coke" to Blackstone "as an elementary work."

4. A recent article, published after the lectures from which these essays are drawn, discusses the work of some judges, from this third period, willing in a related area of tort law to change the common law to the disadvantage of industrialists and entrepreneurs: Peter Karsten, "Explaining the Fight over the Attractive Nuisance Doctrine: A Kinder, Gentler Instrumentalism in the 'Age of Formalism,'" *Law and History Review* 10 (Spring 1992): 45–92.

WILLIAM R. JONES

Sanctuary, Exile, and Law: The Fugitive and Public Authority in Medieval England and Modern America

ON MAY 13, 1497, according to an entry in the sanctuary register of St. Cuthbert's, Durham, a certain Colson of Walsingham, a known thief, escaped from jail and took sanctuary in the cathedral church of Durham, from which he sought deliverance according to an ancient ritual. Standing beside St. Cuthbert's tomb, in the presence of the coroner, the sheriff of Durham, the sacristan, and other witnesses, he confessed his crime and abjured the realm. In the custody of the sheriff and carrying a wooden cross, he was conducted to the king's highway where he was handed over from constable to constable until he reached the nearest port, whence, ostensibly, he departed the land.[1]

Eight centuries before the day on which Colson made his dash to sanctuary, the bishop of Lindisfarne, Cuthbert himself, had on his deathbed warned his fellow monks of the distractions that the presence of his relics would bring to the community from the many fugitives from justice who would flock there seeking sanctuary.[2] The protection that church sanctuary offered fugitive felons was already a venerable institution, and one that had been recognized by Roman emperors and church councils and included in the West Saxon King Ine's code of laws.[3] It survived into the sixteenth century when another English monarch suppressed the great chartered sanctuaries, including the one at Durham, much to the dismay of north country folk to whom it represented a way of life.[4]

As this chronology implies, sanctuary in England has a history extending from late antiquity to the early modern period. It spans the millennium when England transformed itself from a society governed by a folk law of private vengeance and compensation to a society that had begun to submit itself to the transcendent authority of a modern state.

Sanctuary was a cosmopolitan and even universal institution, with counterparts in other religious traditions and earlier cultures. The concept of a sacred space, offering refuge to the persecuted and the pursued, was familiar to the ancient Hebrews, Greeks, and Romans, whose sanctuaries may have inspired similar claims on behalf of Christian churches. The post-Constantinian church of the fourth century was recognized as a specially privileged place. On the other hand, church sanctuary was first mentioned in the edicts of Roman emperors in connection with the intercession of the bishops on behalf of fugitive criminals. Some modern historians have argued that it derived from the church's ministry of compassion, whereby the clergy dispensed *lenitas* or "gentle care" to a vexed and suffering world, rather than from the example of the Jewish city of refuge or the temple asylum of ancient Greece.[5] Roman criminal justice was reluctant to exempt any person or place from its well-regulated world. Roman emperors, while expressing respect for the humanitarian services of the clergy, excluded from the church's protection such unworthy persons as public debtors and traitors. By the early fifth century, however, the sanctity of the interior of Christian churches had been recognized by imperial legislation, which even extended protection to churchyards and adjacent buildings. The aura of holiness, which accrued to churches from the presence of the host and relics of the saints, endowed them with a special status in both secular law and the canons.

The privilege of sanctuary survived the end of Roman rule in Europe. In the early middle ages Germanic law continued to defend the inviolability of churches and the intercessory role of the clergy. For example, the first Christian ruler in England, Ethelbert of Kent, strengthened the protection of the churches of his kingdom by doubling the compensation due for acts of sacrilege.[6] Across the channel in Merovingian Francia, the most notorious wrongdoers were able to escape retribution if they succeeded in reaching a church. The Frankish King Guntram admitted that it would be "impious" to slay an assassin who had to be forced to leave a church.[7] King Childebert, who had been the target of a death plot, promised to spare the lives of the conspirators if they voluntarily left sanctuary: "I am a Christian and I deem it wrong to punish people convicted of a crime if I have to drag them out of a church to do so."[8]

Flight to sanctuary in Anglo-Saxon England occurred against the backdrop of a customary law dependent on self-help, the arbitration of disputes, and the compensation of personal injuries through monetary payments, including what later generations called felonies. Committed to the protection of churches and also to the enforcement of the law of compensation and settlement, English kings from Ethelbert forward intervened to affirm the inviolability of sacred precincts, to define the status of fugitives in churches, and to facilitate the resolution of conflicts by assuring victims of crime and their kin the right to compensation for loss or injury as well as a fine to the king for breach of the peace.[9] Each of these interventions, whether or not they constituted permanent precedents for a royal law of sanctuary, nevertheless, represented the aggrandizement of royal control to the extent that intercession by the king rivaled and even replaced that of the bishop.

For example, Ine of Wessex (688–94), who took a hardline approach to the problem of thievery in his kingdom, spared the lives of those fugitives who sought sanctuary, though they remained subject to the compensation that brought peace in the feud: "If anyone is liable to the death penalty and he reaches a church, he is to retain his life and to compensate as the law directs."[10] In a second sanctuary regulation Ine confirmed the principle of Roman law which allowed the clergy to intervene on behalf of runaway slaves who would be restored to their masters, contingent on the latter's promise to spare them physical punishment: "If anyone is liable to be flogged, and reaches a church, the flogging is to be remitted."[11] Implicit in Ine's legislation was the idea that sanctuary, rather than being an alternative to the law, constituted a means for achieving the goals of settling disputes and restoring peace.

The same rationale underlay the sanctuary laws of King Alfred (871–99). He extended his special protection to all consecrated churches and to certain privileged monastic houses, which were permitted to give temporary refuge to fugitives in the expectation that they would shortly leave sanctuary and be reconciled with their enemies.[12] Accordingly, he forbade the delivery of victuals to persons who ought to stand to justice, while promising them immunity from peremptory retribution if they disarmed and left their churches: "If he himself will hand out his weapons to his foes, they are to keep him for thirty days, and send notice about him to his kinsmen."[13] Further, in order to forestall the outbreak of feuding for undisclosed crimes, Alfred promised to remit half the compensation due from perpetrators who surrendered themselves and confessed.[14] King Ethelstan (924–39), Alfred's grandson, differentiated the degree of protection afforded by various lay and ecclesiastical and personal and territorial authorities, thus indicating the continued importance of intercession in mitigating the harsh penalties of the criminal law.[15]

The mobilization of community resources to pursue fugitives by the hue and cry, even to the extent of besieging the churches in which they took refuge, created a dilemma of law enforcement, which obliged kings to intervene to prevent sacrilege and to temper justice with mercy.[16] In his laws of 1014, King Ethelred (978–1016) distinguished the degree of immunity associated with various religious houses according to a scale of fines reflecting their status in secular law: "All churches are not entitled to the same status in a temporal sense, although they have the same consecration in regard to religion"[17] In another of his sanctuary laws Ethelred exercised his power to grant clemency by commuting the punishment of a person who had fled to sanctuary after committing homicide in another church.[18]

It has been suggested that the outlawry of fugitives in the ninth and tenth centuries complicated the situation with respect to sanctuary: the presence in churches of that special breed of sanctuary seeker, the outlaw, who had already suffered loss of legal rights and confiscation of property by action of a public court, encouraged the king to intervene to protect the right to compensation of victim and kin, and to resolve potentially deadly confrontations, short of allowing a lynch mob to exact the ultimate penalty.[19]

Although there is little evidence to illustrate the actual enforcement of Anglo-Saxon sanctuary law, it is clear that the objective of English kings was to accommodate it to the folk law, which was the final resort against crime and feuding. In the process of accomplishing this goal, they transformed the role of sanctuary in the system of criminal justice and, most important, used it to enhance the discretionary authority of the king. By granting special protection to persons and places, by commuting the punishment of certain crimes and by making sanctuary an opportunity for settling disputes, they contributed to the expansion of that public sphere of justice that modern historians have recognized as an important aspect of the growth of preconquest kingship.[20]

Anglo-Norman and Angevin kings of the twelfth and thirteenth centuries succeeded in replacing the folk law implicating the victim as an active participant in the prosecution of crime. They introduced a new criminal justice system based on a monopoly of criminal prosecutions by the king's courts, the restriction of private appeals of felony, and the extension of the concept of the king's peace to the entire kingdom.

The most important procedural innovation in the history of sanctuary in England appeared in the latter part of Henry I's reign (1100–35), and played a vital role in this process. Its earliest mention is in the apocryphal tract, "The Laws of Edward the Confessor," which apparently dates from about 1130–35. In a brief list of sanctuary rules, which are mainly concerned with regulating access to churches, the anonymous author described the procedure for dealing with the professional thief who was in the process of becoming a professional sanctuary seeker: "If, however, he has done this repeatedly and happens to take refuge repeatedly in this way, after restoring what he has stolen, he shall abjure the province and shall not return (*ablatione reddita, provinciam forisiuret nec redeat*). And if he should return let no one dare to receive him, save by the leave of the justices of the lord king."[21]

This laconic statement contains the earliest reference to the sentence of abjuration instituted by royal authority in order to rid churches of repeat offenders in sanctuary. Although the author calls for the restitution of ill-gotten gains, we hear nothing of the old system of compensation. Rather, the king, through his justices, grants clemency and banishes the culprit from the district. The procedure of abjuration implied the application of the king's power to commute the capital sentence required by law. Its adoption constituted another step in the establishment of the king's exclusive authority to arbitrate in the realm of criminal justice. Subsequently extended to the nation at large, probably on the model of outlawry, it represented, as did outlawry, a procedure uniquely royal in origin and intent. Its usefulness in dealing with other notorious and inveterate malefactors is suggested by the author's recommendation that it be applied in the cases of pardoned murderers as well as convicted felons who were unable to provide pledges for their future good conduct.[22] Viewed from the perspective of the growth of English criminal justice, abjuration of the realm signaled the transition from a legal order—wherein the king intervened in pleas of sanctuary to facilitate the settlement of disputes—to one in which he alone exacted the state's toll for crime.

Equally central to the process of institutionalizing sanctuary privilege in criminal justice administration was the creation of the office of the coroner—the royal official specifically assigned to deliver churches of fugitive felons. "The Laws of Edward the Confessor" had stated that only the "king's justices" might allow abjurors to return to the scenes of their crimes. It is possible that as early as the late Saxon period a royal official had negotiated the surrender of fugitives from churches.[23] Well before the establishment in 1194 of the office of the coroner, other royal officials such as the county justiciars under Henry I and the hundred bailiffs of Henry II's reign (1154–89) had performed these duties.[24] The coroner, elected by the county or town, or appointed by franchise holders, was responsible for "keeping the pleas of the Crown," including the abjurations of persons in sanctuary. Responsible also for holding inquests on dead bodies, receiving confessions and the appeals of approvers, and organizing outlawries, the coroner became the king's principal agent for all matters touching sanctuary. He also received custody of fugitives willing to submit to trial or received their abjurations, drafted their itineraries out of the country, and orchestrated the ceremonies involving the four neighboring townships and local officials who witnessed these events and were expected to attend the inquest into the chattels of abjurors.[25]

The coroner's roll, in which were recorded confessions and abjurations, was a record at law, useful for checking information presented by jurors in the county courts or before the justices itinerant. By the creation of the office of the coroner and its assumption of responsibility for the oversight of sanctuary privilege, the king had made the church's claim to immunize fugitive felons from the full effects of the law a matter of royal grace. The king substituted for bishop and priest his own intermediary in the person of the coroner.

The plea of sanctuary and the procedure for delivering churches of fugitive felons were improvised over the twelfth century. The earliest recorded cases of abjuration appear in coroners' rolls of the thirteenth century. The first explicit description of the fully articulated procedure for abjuring the realm is contained in Henry de Bracton's book *On the Laws and Customs of England,* written about the middle of the thirteenth century. Bracton identified as one of the "Pleas of the Crown" the quasi-judicial procedure whereby a fugitive was given the choice of exiting the church to stand trial in a royal court, or of confessing his crime and swearing to abjure the realm.[26] His scenario of the procedure became sufficiently authoritative that it was later excerpted and copies circulated as official "statutes."[27] It is recognizable as the procedure imposed in the case of Colson of Walsingham centuries afterward, although Colson's flight from jail, to sanctuary, and thence to the king's highway, occurred within a single day. Also, Colson abjured the kingdom from one of England's great chartered churches.

There was always variation in practice from place to place—the product of local custom or special privilege.[28] For example, Bracton had insisted that convicted felons or fugitives caught red-handed with stolen property should not enjoy the forty-day grace period before having to decide their fate, although this period of respite became customary for all sanctuary seekers in the course of the thirteenth century. The opinion of legal experts differed, however, as to when exactly the forty-day breathing period began—upon the fugitive's entry into sanctuary or from the time of the coroner's arrival. Further, Bracton had argued that abjurors should be allowed to choose their ports of departure, whereas it became customary for coroners to assign them. Nor was every abjuror accompanied, as was Colson on his march to the sea, by a succession of constables providing escort to a seaport or to one of the Welsh or Scottish border towns. Finally, a protracted debate occurred between common lawyers and canonists and among judges and various lay and clerical authorities as to whether it was necessary to confess to a felony in order to claim sanctuary, or whether it also covered trespass and debt. The law was very definite, however, as to the peremptory execution by beheading or hanging, which awaited the abjuror who strayed from his route out of the country or who dared to return without the king's pardon.

It is, of course, very unlikely that most abjurors actually departed the kingdom. Once out of sight of victims and neighbors, they could easily disappear into the landscape. Given the limited ability of medieval legal administration to enforce even its most solemn judgments, the best that could be hoped for was that the identities of abjurors would be publicized as widely as possible. The ceremony of abjuration served to disseminate knowledge of confessed criminals throughout the neighboring townships. Information contained in the coroner's rolls was available to the public courts. As was so often the case with medieval law-enforcement, authorities had to be satisfied with naming public enemies and warning them to keep their distance.[29]

The procedure of abjuration was unique to medieval England and the duchy of Normandy where it was introduced by Anglo-Norman dukes.[30] Norman practice varied from the English by limiting the grace period to eight days rather than the forty of English usage, and by employing officials other than the coroner to receive abjurations. From Bracton's time, medieval and modern commentators alike have been curious as to the origin of the distinctive English technique for ridding the nation of public nuisances. In a badly muddled paraphrase of the Roman jurist Marcion's classic exposition of the three kinds of "exile" known to Roman law-*interdictio, relegatio,* and *deportatio*—Bracton drew the analogy between abjuration and outlawry: "exclusion from certain places . . . for ever or for a time . . . exclusion from all places except [a certain place] forever, or deportation to an island, forever or for a time, which may be termed abjuration of the realm or outlawry (*abiuratio regni sive utlagatio*)."[31] The majority of modern historians of sanctuary have followed Bracton in seeing it as an "offshoot" of the process of outlawry and, thus, assumed its unique English origin.[32] Although the evidence is meager and ambiguous, there is, however, some suggestion that the banishment of fugitives had precedents in Romanized versions of continental Germanic legal procedure. It is clear that the "exile" of sanctuary seekers as an alternative to death or mutilation was an accepted punishment in early medieval Europe.

The classic Roman law of exile was, at its inception in the republic, virtually a birthright of patrician citizens seeking to escape judgment in the public courts. It was transformed into a terrible weapon of autocracy by early emperors.[33] Its complex distinctions and gradations, intimately connected with Roman jurisprudence and political culture, were abandoned in the barbarian world of the early middle ages. But the name, *exilium,* and the penalties of banishment and confiscation of property were retained by Germanic kings as punishment for their enemies and as appropriate for certain crimes.

For example, Visigothic law decreed the exile of persons guilty of slaying a parent.[34] Roman Burgundian law exiled false accusers in the courts.[35] Roman legal history itself left a precedent for the exile of a particularly notorious criminal, who had taken refuge in a church in Milan in 396, and who was saved from being devoured by wild beasts by a timely divine intervention.[36] Later, in Ostrogothic Italy, Theodoric had exiled a fugitive who had taken sanctuary.[37] The Frankish ruler Childebert exiled two would-be assassins whom he had enticed out of a church.[38] In the few cases where the evidence is explicit, it appears that banishment was accompanied by the confiscation of personal property, which, it is known, was a practice of the Roman law of exile.[39]

The Carolingian dynasty was determined to enforce law and order throughout the Frankish kingdom. Charlemagne, while showing respect for sanctuary, intervened to prevent feuding, to assure the compensation of victims of crime, and to assert the royal right to punish or to pardon. The Saxon capitulary of 785 promised sanctuary seekers, excepting only robbers and arsonists of churches, that their lives would be spared if they surrendered, compensated their victims, and submitted to royal judgment:

> If anyone seeks refuge in a church, no one should attempt to expel him by force, but he should be permitted to have his peace until he presents himself to judgment; and his life should be spared in honor of God and Holy Church. But he should amend his crimes so far as he can and as it shall be determined; and he should then be conducted into the presence of the lord king who may send him wheresoever he pleases (*et sic ducatur ad praesentiam domni regis; et ipsi eum mittat ubi clementiae ipsius placuerit*).[40]

It appears that Charles agreed with Pope Leo III, who had counseled him to substitute sentence of exile for the punishment of death or mutilation that awaited fugitives in sanctuary.[41] But it is also clear that the emperor intended to regulate this matter by reserving to himself final authority over the disposition of the persons of such malefactors.[42] That sentence of exile had the added virtue of curtailing the dreary cycle of retaliation and revenge was implied by a capitulary of 819, which aimed at preventing murder.[43] The banishment of criminals, which was a weapon of sovereign authority, tended to devolve upon the greater provincial lords, who were the heirs of the Carolingians in the anarchy that followed the breakup of the Frankish kingdom. Upwardly mobile Norman dukes of the tenth century coped with the anomic violence of their homeland by augmenting the spiritual sanctions of the church against violators of the peace of God, through proclamations of the ducal ban with its threat of exile and confiscation.[44]

Exile of the Roman variety was unknown in medieval England.[45] On those occasions when Anglo-Saxon kings threatened malefactors with expulsion from their places of residence, they clearly aimed to rid the countryside of certain categories of socially unacceptable persons. For instance, King Wihtred of Kent (795) ordered all foreigners guilty of adultery to quit the kingdom.[46] By a joint decree, King Edward, Alfred's son, and the Danish chieftain Guthrum commanded that the land be "purified" of sorcerers, perjurers, assassins, and prostitutes.[47] King Ethelstan threatened to relocate to other parts of his kingdom members of powerful and wealthy clans who consistently violated their oaths to keep the peace.[48] He also ordered notorious troublemakers to be driven from their "native districts" with "their wives and cattle" in the event they did not mend their ways.[49] Finally, the laws of Cnut in the early eleventh century attempted to enforce the penitential doctrine of Wulfstan and his circle by ordering priests guilty of homicide to undertake a pilgrimage at the pope's behest.[50] He also declared that the murderers of priests atone for their sins in exile.[51] This abrupt and wholesale expulsion of undesirables and Cnut's association of the discomfort of exile with penance and atonement were, however, very different from the judicial exile practiced by continental kings. The absence in English law of the confiscation of personal property also implied a difference from procedures followed abroad.

Some eleventh-century Norman sources equate the Norman equivalent of outlawry, the ducal "foreban," with a sentence of exile.[52] By Bracton's time, however, the two are clearly distinguished in both English and Norman law. The thirteenth-century *Summa de Legibus Normanniae* underscored the difference between a capital sentence (*aut per corporis destructionem*), banishment (*vel per forisbannitionem*), and abjuration (*vel per patrie abjurationem*).[53] The same distinctions were made by English jurists.[54] Further, abjuration and outlawry had come to differ in their intent. Abjuration constituted an alternative to trial in a royal court available to a confessed felon who, however, remained within the king's protection after confession but prior to his departure from the realm. By contrast, outlawry was a process of judicial intimidation aimed at forcing fugitives to come to justice if they would avoid the consequences of their contempt. In one sense, both the abjuror and the outlaw were in contempt of the king's justice because of their refusal to submit. The confiscation of property in both cases probably suggested their similarity. But the seizure of the lands and chattels of outlaws was a final punishment for contumacy. Confiscation of the goods of abjurors and the waste of their lands for a year and a day represented the punishment meted out to confessed felons.[55]

Procedures for extracting fugitives from sanctuary in continental Europe have not been as fully investigated as has the English practice of abjuration. In France, Germany, and the Lowlands from the thirteenth through the fifteenth centuries, however, fugitives in churches, who refused to submit to secular justice, were sentenced to banishment.[56] As a prerogative of sovereign authority, banishment was proclaimed in the name of the principal governor, whether the king, a feudal magnate, or a municipality. Out of respect for ecclesiastical immunity, the banishment of clerics was recognized to pertain to the bishop or his representative. Like outlawry, banishment entailed the loss of civil rights and the confiscation of personal property. It was viewed as constituting the ultimate punishment for contempt.[57] Persons under such disabilities were denied access to sanctuary. In the course of arguing a sensational sanctuary case in the late fifteenth century, the procurator of the king of France described the status of a victim of banishment as comparable to that of the slave, the outlaw, and the exile: "*est quasi-servus, penae ascriptus et subditus, habitans extra regnum et exclusus ab habitatione regni.*"[58] Pardon, in the form of a letter of remission was, of course, available from the authority that had pronounced sentence of banishment. During the late middle ages it is likely that banishment became increasingly appealing to fugitives who found the protection of churches less certain.[59]

The author of the "Laws of Edward the Confessor" in the twelfth century had suggested multiple uses for the oath of abjuration. It could be required of pardoned murderers, convicted felons who could not provide pledges for their future conduct, and recidivist sanctuary seekers. In the course of explaining the origin of the forty-day grace period claimed by fugitives to sanctuary, Bracton identified another of its applications, when he observed that Henry II's Assize of Clarendon (1166) had allowed this period of time to certain accused felons in order that they might seek the assistance of kinfolk and friends prior to their enforced departure from the kingdom.[60] The Assize had required the abjuration of persons indicted for major crimes—murder, theft, robbery, counterfeiting, and arson—who, although they had successfully performed the ordeal as proof of their innocence, nevertheless remained suspect of these crimes in the opinion of reliable local jurors. Accordingly, in the event the accused was unable to provide pledges, he should "go out of the kingdom within forty days and take with him his chattels, saving the rights of his lords; and let him abjure the realm [on pain of being] in the king's mercy (*infra quadraginta dies a regno exeat et catalla sua secum asportet, salvo iure dominorum suorum, et regnum abiuret in misericordia domini regis*)."[61]

Substantial proof that the king's courts were requiring felons to abjure, despite their success at the ordeal, is provided by court rolls of the late twelfth and early thirteenth centuries. Persons indicted of major crimes by the jurors' testimony in the hundreds and vills were subsequently adjudged guilty by the "medial" verdict of the same jurors on the presumption of their guilt by notoriety or specific inculpatory evidence.[62] In the absence of the formal trial jury, which did not appear until 1215, when the pope forbade clerics to participate in ordeals, the simultaneous accusation and conviction of the perpetrators of major crimes produced a group of undesirables for which enforced exile seemed appropriate. In short, abjuration served to rid the nation of both the "convicted" felons of the assize and the "confessed" felons who left sanctuary.

After 1215 and the introduction of the criminal trial jury, abjuration was most often confined to sanctuary seekers who chose to avoid trial in the royal courts. Yet it remained an alternative or added punishment for persons whose continued presence was viewed as a threat to public safety. King John, for example, followed the recommendation of the "Laws of Edward the Confessor" and forced pardoned murderers to abjure.[63] Abjuration was mentioned in the famous "due process" clause of Magna Carta.[64] Pardoned thieves abjured the realm in the thirteenth century[65] Henry III's forest charter (1217) imposed it on trespassers in the royal forest who, after temporary imprisonment, failed to produce pledges.[66] Edward I substituted it for the death penalty in the case of a cleric who introduced a papal bull contrary to the interests of the king and kingdom.[67] The second Statute of Westminister (1285) enforced it as an alternative to the perpetual confinement of kidnappers.[68] There were a number of sensational cases of "political exile" in the late middle ages.[69] But England never matched the number of exiles that the Renaissance Italian cities dispatched to those "Contrary Commonwealths" described by Randolph Starn.[70] Finally, abjuration and exile had a longer history in English criminal justice procedure than is generally appreciated. Jesuits, for instance, abjured the realm during the Reformation, and major criminals were deported abroad in the eighteenth century.[71]

All consecrated churches, monastic houses, cemeteries, and the barns, granges, and dwellings of the clergy were recognized as capable of granting sanctuary. This status was defended by sentences of automatic excommunication against violators. The grant by kings and popes of special privileges to certain religious houses and the acquisition of vast franchisal immunities by churches and prelates created enclaves that were not subject to intervention by secular authority. In England some two dozen or so great churches were specially privileged by royal and papal charters. Some of these claimed sanctuary jurisdiction extending a mile around the principal church. This area was divided into concentric zones for assessing the fines imposed on intruders as they approached the main altar.[72]

Other chartered sanctuary churches had facilities for domiciling, feeding, and clothing inmates on a long-term or permanent basis. A few even sought to integrate sanctuary seekers into the devotional and social life of the community by requiring an oath of allegiance and the promise of good conduct.[73] St. John's, Beverley, and St. Cuthbert's, Durham, enjoyed liberal privileges and national clienteles.[74] The Cistercian houses of northern England were so thoroughly integrated into the life of the march that Archbishop Edward Lee of York complained to Cromwell that their closure was an affront to the culture of his parishioners.[75] The exaggerated rights claimed by the London sanctuaries of St. Peter's, Westminster, and St. Martin le Grand, which were especially receptive to fleeing debtors, were sources of continuing friction with the kings, municipal authorities, and city guilds.[76]

It is impossible to estimate precisely the number of persons who took sanctuary and abjured the realm during the English middle ages. One impressionistic modern estimate holds that perhaps a thousand persons annually sought the church's protection in this way.[77] James Given has calculated that 7.4 percent, or 258 of the 3,492 homicide cases that he analyzed from plea rolls of the first half of the thirteenth century involved fugitives who abjured the realm. He projected cases in the "thousands" for the thirteenth and fourteenth centuries.[78] There was considerable variation from place to place. Twenty persons took sanctuary in Staffordshire during the first year of Edward I's reign. But the average was about thirty for each seven-year period in thirteenth-century Sussex.[79] The more precise statistics provided by the sanctuary registers of Beverley and Durham are not at all representative of England in general.

One thing is clear, however; the overwhelming majority of sanctuary seekers were male, because it was the masculine part of the population that went armed and sometimes used its weapons, engaged in trade and incurred debt, and composed that huge community of thieves and robbers, the bane of medieval life. Yet numbers alone do not explain the importance of sanctuary in the jurisdictional relations of church and state in medieval England. Situated as it was on the border between church and state, sanctuary could easily become a source of contention between religious authorities who took seriously their ministry of compassion and secular officials intent on protecting public safety.

It is evident from parliamentary petitions and statutes, clerical grievances, and the decisions of common lawyers and canonists that both king and community as well as church and state looked to secular authority for the defense and regulation of sanctuary. In 1257, on the occasion of a request for a clerical subsidy, prelates complained to Henry III concerning the too close confinement of fugitives in churches and their violent removal or malicious enticement from sanctuary. The result was that the "custom of the realm," which gave them forty-days grace and the right to abjure, was contravened.[80] Writing later in the thirteenth century concerning the popularity of Cistercian houses as places of refuge, Archbishop John Pecham characterized sanctuary as almost a matter of royal grace: "For to the Crown belongs not only cruelty and rigor of justice, but still more pity and mercy. By which the Holy Church, by the King's will, saves evildoers by sanctuary of the Church."[81]

The idea that sanctuary was as much a concession of the crown as a right of the church was implicit in Edward I's grant in 1284 of sanctuary privilege to the people of the newly conquered principality of Wales.[82] By statute of 1315–16, Edward II declared that the "custom of the realm," which allowed fugitives to abjure, should be respected, and that abjurors traveling the king's highway were to be regarded as "in the king's peace."[83] The frequency with which litigants and petitioners addressed complaints for or against sanctuary to the king indicates the consensus of opinion that it lay within his power to regulate it. The right of the sovereign to decide the legitimacy of pleas of sanctuary, in particular instances, rested on ancient precedents extending back to the times of Theodosius, Justinian, and Charlemagne.[84]

During the Middle Ages both church and state concurred in denying the church's protection to such enemies of public order as highwaymen, brigands, assassins, perpetrators of sacrilege, or felons who used sanctuary to commit other crimes.[85] But the claim of sanctuary for debt was the subject of a protracted debate in medieval England. In response to the appeals of creditors, statutes of Edward III and Richard II prohibited the use of sanctuary by fraudulent debtors. The new laws provided for the collection of legitimate debts by exactions on the property of sanctuary seekers.[86] In 1378, on the occasion of a scandalous breach of sanctuary at Westminster, the question of sanctuary for debt was debated by common lawyers and canonists in Parliament itself.[87] Access to churches by fugitive debtors was never wholly eliminated. The London sanctuaries of Westminster and St. Martin le Grand were virtual nests of such crooks as late as the fifteenth century. Nevertheless, the king's claim to approve the privilege in particular instances was a weapon to be held in reserve, and to be used to chip away at sanctuary privilege when he chose to do so.

Until late in its history, the principle underlying sanctuary was seldom disputed. Controversy centered, rather, on cases of its violation or abuse. Medieval canon law had established the theoretical immunity of churches from intrusion by secular authority. Medieval kings generally respected the church's claims. When royal officials or royal rights and revenues were put in jeopardy, however, the king could be expected to react. There was nothing inevitable nor invariable in the conflict of church and state over sanctuary. English kings of the Middle Ages showed their willingness to recognize the liberties of the church by restoring fugitives who had been unlawfully removed from sanctuary, by forbidding the compulsory abjuration of clerics contrary to benefit of clergy, and by punishing their own officials for overenthusiastic law-enforcement practices.[88] Even during the Tudor period, when sanctuary came under attack from skeptical royal judges and hostile municipal officials, there was a reluctance to abandon an institution hallowed by law, custom, and religious idealism. Temporal and spiritual authorities generally cooperated to enforce the criminal law while admitting the church's right to mitigate its effects.

As was the case with respect to other areas of enforced cooperation between the two jurisdictions—benefit of clergy and the caption of excommunicates—a high degree of mutual respect, forbearance, and compromise was necessary to avoid conflict. Over its long history, sanctuary had to accommodate to changing political structures, juridical systems, and legal norms. By means of a series of procedural innovations, which constituted theoretical accretions of power to the crown, public authority in England managed to capture the plea of sanctuary for its courts. The cumulative effect of royal intervention in the operation of sanctuary was to transform an institution that was symbolic of the church's moral and legal autonomy into a vehicle for the enforcement of the state's jurisdiction over criminals and crime.

From the late fifteenth into the sixteenth and seventeenth centuries, the political and legal environment in which sanctuary existed was profoundly altered in response to the challenges of Tudor and Stuart statecraft and the opposition to ecclesiastical immunity implicit in the new reformed religion. The same distrust of exemptions from royal justice and the common law that underlay the attack on feudal liberties and hostility toward the separate polities of Wales and Ireland, also prompted the council and the king's courts to view with a heightened skepticism some of the more exaggerated pretensions of ecclesiastical jurisdiction. The king's criminal courts were particularly aggressive in scrutinizing the claims of chartered sanctuaries. The highly visible and controversial London sanctuaries of Westminister and St. Martin le Grand were subjected to proof of their rights by the exacting standards of possession of sealed royal charters, lengthy usage, and allowance of their claims in general eyre.[89] Since most of the "ancient" charters were later forgeries and because it was in practice difficult to demonstrate allowance of claims by royal judges, the churches were at a serious disadvantage in proving their rights at law.

Even though sanctuary was not abolished until 1624, the Tudors imposed tighter regulations on it by restricting the types of crimes it covered, by experimenting with alternatives to it, and by questioning the rationale on which it was based. By a statute of 1524 Henry VIII marked the bodies of abjurors with a distinguishing brand, as a few years later he marked them with an identifying badge.[90] The parliamentary session of 1530–31, expressing alarm at a loss of military expertise abroad caused by the abjuration of soldiers and sailors, abolished abjuration of the realm, thus effectively transforming would-be abjurors into prisoners for life.[91] In 1534 traitors were excluded from the privilege, thereby realizing a goal that dated back to the accession of the dynasty.[92] Finally, the statute of 1540 swept away the chartered sanctuaries, leaving only the consecrated churches of parish and diocese as havens of refuge. It excluded from enjoyment of the privilege all persons accused of the commission of a felony, who henceforth were required to "abjure" the local churches to take up residence in certain cities of refuge, which the government established across the country. Because, as the preamble to the statute declared, sanctuary had operated "to the greate displeasure of Allmighty God & to the subversion of all good and politicke ordre," persons accused of serious crimes were relegated to strict confinement in certain designated municipalities where their future conduct could be regulated.[93]

There was a growing tendency to discuss sanctuary in terms of first principles. As early as 1399 some royal judges had expressed opposition to the creation of new sanctuaries on the grounds that the king could not grant away his power to pardon. Later generations of English jurists denied that the monarch had the authority to admit debtors and traitors to sanctuary.[94] But the most famous discussion of the theory of sanctuary appeared in the speech which Sir Thomas More put in the mouth of the duke of Buckingham in his life of Richard III.[95] The plea of sanctuary, Buckingham argued, represented an unwarranted exception to the legitimate pardoning power of the crown. Implicit in Buckingham's tirade was the idea that whatever usefulness sanctuary may once have had for tempering justice with mercy, at this late date it had become a hindrance to the proper administration of the criminal law and an unnecessary alternative to the royal right to pardon criminals.

From the perspective of Europe in general, sanctuary was on the defensive throughout the early modern period. Protestant nations, suspicious of the pretensions of the medieval church, quietly abandoned it. Even Catholic Europe narrowed its scope, reduced its coverage, and subordinated its application to the agenda of public justice.[96] The geographical extent of sanctuary was restricted to the interiors of churches. The list of excluded crimes was considerably lengthened, often with the concurrence of the papacy and the national hierarchies. The French ordinance of Villers-Cotterets became a model for other states seeking to limit the privilege. It abolished sanctuary for civil cases and drastically curtailed its role in criminal matters by allowing the "preliminary extraction" of fugitives and their detention in prison until the secular power had determined the validity of the claim in particular instances. Even the canonists, who published extensive scholarly commentaries on the privilege, seemed to lost confidence in it. Some even questioned its divine origin.

In a series of ordinances and concordats of the seventeenth and eighteenth centuries, the right to sanctuary was gradually eliminated as an adjunct or accessory of continental criminal justice. Severely restricted in its application, sanctuary was tolerated in some parts of southern and eastern Europe into the nineteenth century. When its end finally arrived, it was not with a bang but a whimper. What become of the Catholic Church's final word on the subject appears in the canon law code of 1917, which declared that "a church enjoys the right of asylum, so that guilty persons who take refuge in it must not be taken from it, except in the case of necessity, without the consent of the ordinary, or at least of the rector of the church."[97] The justification for intervention by "necessity" and the limiting of the church's role to the giving of the bishop's or priest's "consent" effectively eliminated sanctuary as a bar to the operation of sovereign criminal justice. Even this timid defense was not dignified by inclusion in the revised code of 1983.[98] The few sanctuary claims in present-day Ireland and in Manuel Noriega's Panama do not indicate confidence in the institution.

Church sanctuary disappeared as a legal and historical reality, surviving as a romantic memory in literature, legend, and art. The centrist regimes of the modern era were intolerant of the existence of exceptions of any kind to their own courts, laws, and constabularies. Immunities and exemptions, whether feudal, municipal, or ecclesiastical, collapsed and were reabsorbed into the jurisdictions of sovereign states, which imposed on their citizenry the duty of total conformity with national law and justice. In the sixteenth century Jean Bodin, who equated sovereignty itself with the rules of a unitary law, had recommended that states cooperate in the suppression of crime. The founders of international law, Grotius and Pufendorf, argued that nations might refuse admission to fugitive criminals and repatriate them to their native lands for punishment.[99]

Although the idea of asylum for the victims of religious and political persecution emerged during the Enlightenment and the revolutionary period, this principle was honored more by philosophers than by politicians and lawyers. From its very beginning, international law was more a law of sovereign states than of individual human rights. This fact shaped the refugee and asylum policies, and the immigration and naturalization laws of Europe and America well into the twentieth century.[100] Even after the assimilation of U.S. refugee policy began to conform to international standards of humanitarianism in 1980, the admission of refugees was normally dictated by considerations of foreign policy, national security, economic necessity, or racial preference. Further, discretionary authority with respect to the admission, rejection, or extradiction and repatriation of refugees was vested in the executive branch. The system operated, it has been said, in ways curiously unaffected by those principles of due process and judicial equity that had transformed other areas of American law.[101]

On two occasions in the second half of the twentieth century, American political activists resurrected sanctuary as a way for expressing disapproval of American foreign policy and its defense by American courts. A native tradition of civil disobedience, with roots in abolitionism and the underground railroad, energized the antiwar movement of the 1960s and the sanctuary movement of the 1980s.[102] Although church sanctuary has no standing in American law and only a nominal significance in modern Roman Catholicism, the name and the theory of sanctuary were revived to protest American policy in Vietnam and to publicize the plight of Central American refugees.[103] In both instances groups of American citizens engaged in acts of civil disobedience to oppose U.S. foreign policy by breaking the laws that sanctioned it.

The connection between medieval sanctuary and its modern version was, however, tenuous. In the modern American sanctuary movements, persons other than members of the clergy and institutions other than churches were involved as participants. Their supporters readily admitted that sanctuary for draft resisters or illegal aliens was more a symbolic gesture than a legally defensible act. Although some learned and eloquent arguments for the continuity of sanctuary from medieval England to modern America have been published, the two were fundamentally different in nature and intent.[104] Modern sanctuary movements are political initiatives directed against established policy and law, whereas medieval church sanctuary was an institutionalized adjunct of criminal justice. The more persuasive analogy is probably that which can be drawn between the humanitarian services offered by modern "sanctuary workers" to conscientious objectors and undocumented aliens. The church's ministry of compassion may indeed have been the origin of sanctuary itself.

NOTES

1. James Raine, ed., *Sanctuarium Dunelmense et Beverlacense,* Publication of the Surtees Society V (London: J. N. B. Nichols & Son, 1837), 30–31.

2. Bede, "Life of Cuthbert," *Lives of the Saints,* J. F. Webb, ed. (Harmondsworth and New York: Penguin Books, 1965), 119: "They will flee for refuge to my body, for, whatever I might be, my fame as a servant of God has been noised abroad. You will be constrained to intercede very often with the powers of this world on behalf of such men. The presence of my remains will prove extremely irksome."

3. Dorothy Whitelock, ed., *English Historical Documents, c. 500–1042* (New York: Oxford University Press, 1955), 365 (Ine, 5).

4. J. Charles Cox, *The Sanctuaries and Sanctuary Seekers of Mediaeval England* (London: George Allen & Sons, 1911), 161. Archbishop Edward Lee of York writing in 1536 to Thomas Cromwell about the closing of the sanctuary at Hexham: "And what comfort that monasteries is daily to the country there, and specially in time of war, not only the country men do know, but also many of the noble men of this realm."

5. Pierre Timbal Duclaux de Martin, *Le droit d'asile* (Paris: Librairie du Recueil Sirey, 1939), 32–92; G. Le Bras, "Asile," *Dictionnaire d'histoire et de géographie ecclésiastiques,* A. Baudrillart, A. de Meyer and Et. van Cauwenbergh, eds. (Paris: Librairie Letouzey

et Ané, 1930), IV, cols. 1035–38; E. Herman, "Asile dans l'église orientale," *Dictionnaire du droit canonique,* R. Naz, ed. (Paris: Librairie Letouzey et Ané, 1935), I, cols. 1084–85.

6. Whitelock, *Historical Documents,* 357 (Ethelbert, 1).

7. Gregory of Tours, *The History of the Franks,* Lewis Thorpe, ed. (Harmondsworth and Baltimore: Penguin Books, 1974), 482 (IX, 3).

8. Ibid., 525 (IX, 38).

9. For the analysis of sanctuary legislation in the context of Anglo-Saxon folk law, see Charles E. Riggs, Jr., *Criminal Asylum in Anglo-Saxon Law,* University of Florida Monographs: Social Sciences 18 (Gainesville: University of Florida Press, 1963). The older works on sanctuary in England are weak on the earlier period, but useful as guides to the sources for the later Middle Ages. See Norman Maclaren Trenholme, *The Right of Sanctuary in England: A Study in Institutional History,* University of Missouri Studies, vol. I, no. 5 (Columbia: University of Missouri, 1903); Thomas John de' Mazzinghi, *Sanctuaries* (Stafford: Halden & Son, 1987); Cox, *Sanctuaries and Sanctuary Seekers.*

10. F. L. Attenborough, ed., *The Laws of the Earliest English Kings* (1922; reprint, New York: Russell & Russell, 1963), 39 (Ine, 5).

11. Ibid., (Ine, 5.1).

12. Whitelock, *Historical Documents,* 374–75 (Alfred, 2, 5, 5.1).

13. Ibid., 375 (Alfred, 5.3).

14. Ibid. (Alfred, 5.3).

15. Attenborough, *Laws,* 149 (Ethelstan, 6.1, 6.2, 6.3).

16. Riggs, *Criminal Asylum,* 17–19.

17. Whitelock, *Historical Documents,* 411 (Ethelred, 5).

18. Ibid. (Ethelred, 1).

19. Riggs, *Criminal Asylum,* 40–50.

20. Naomi D. Hurnard, *The King's Pardon for Homicide Before A.D. 1307* (Oxford: Clarendon Press, 1969), 1–5; Patrick Wormald, "Charters, Law and the Settlement of Disputes in Anglo-Saxon England," *The Settlement of Disputes in Early Modern Europe,* Wendy Davies and Paul Fouracre, eds. (Cambridge: Cambridge University Press, 1986), 167; "Conclusion," 229.

21. F. Liebermann, ed., *Die Gesetze der Angelsachsen* (Halle: Max Niemeyer, 1903), I/3, 630 (5.3); Riggs, *Criminal Asylum,* 48 n. 22.

22. Liebermann, *Gesetze,* I/3, 643 (18.a); 644 (18.2); Hurnard, *King's Pardon,* 15.

23. Riggs, *Criminal Asylum,* 19.

24. R. F. Hunnisett, *The Medieval Coroner* (Cambridge: Cambridge University Press, 1961), 1–3.

25. Ibid., 37–54.

26. Henry de Bracton, *On the Laws and Customs of England,* trans. Samuel E. Thorne (Cambridge: Belknap Press, 1968), II, 382–84.

27. Edw. I., Off. Coronatoris, *Statutes of the Realm,* I, 40–41.

28. Compare *Britton,* trans. Francis Morgan Nichols (Oxford: Clarendon Press, 1865), I, 62–66; *Fleta,* H. G. Richardson and G. O. Sayles, eds., Selden Society 7 (London: Bernard Quaritch, 1955), II, 76–77.

29. H. R. T. Summerson, "The Structure of Law Enforcement in Thirteenth Century England," *American Journal of Legal History* 23 (1979): 313–27.

30. André Réville, "L'Abjuratio Regni": histoire d'une institution anglaise," *Révue historique* 50 (1892): 1–42.

31. Bracton, *Laws and Customs,* II, 383–84.

32. Réville, "Abjuratio Regni," 5–7, 9; Timbal Duclaux de Martin, *Droit d'asile,* 240–41; Trenholme, *Right of Sanctuary,* 16–17.

33. James Strachan-Davidson, *Problems of the Roman Criminal Law* (1912; reprint, Oxford: Clarendon Press, 1969), II, 24–30, 51–74.

34. L. F. Misserey, "Asile en occident," *Dictionnaire du droit canonique,* I, 1089.

35. Julius Goebel, Jr., *Felony and Misdemeanor: A Study in the History of the Criminal Law* (Philadelphia: University of Pennsylvania Press, 1937), 59.

36. Timbal Duclaux de Martin, *Droit d'asile,* 62.

37. Ibid., 107.

38. Gregory of Tours, *History of the Franks,* 525.

39. Goebel, *Felony and Misdemeanor,* 54–59.

40. G. H. Pertz, ed., *Monumenta Germaniae Historica: Legum* (1835; reprint, Vaduz: 1965), I, 48.

41. Timbal Duclaux de Martin, *Droit d'asile,* 141 n. 4.

42. Pertz, *Legum,* I, 113.

43. J. J. E. Proost, *Histoire du droit d'asile religieux en Belgique* (Gand: Hebbelynck, 1870), 19.

44. Goebel, *Felony and Misdemeanor,* 310–12.

45. Frederick Pollock and Frederic William Maitland, *The History of English Law before the Time of Edward I,* 2d ed. (Cambridge: Cambridge University Press, 1899), II, 518.

46. Attenborough, *Laws,* 25 (Wihtred, 3).

47. Ibid., 109 (Edward and Guthrum, 11).

48. Ibid., 145 (III Ethelstan, 6).

49. Ibid., 147 (IV Ethelstan, 3); 153 (V Ethelstan, 1).

50. Riggs, *Criminal Asylum,* 50–54.

51. Whitelock, *Historical Documents,* 420 (Cnut, 6); 424 (Cnut, 39).

52. Goebel, *Felony and Misdemeanor,* 312 n. 94.

53. Ibid., 278 n. 204.

54. Trenholme, *Right of Sanctuary,* 43–44, citing *Rotuli Parliamentorum,* I, 52b, on the three writs of escheat: *Quia utlagatus, vel suspensus, vel quis abjuravit regnum.*

55. John Bellamy, *Crime and Public Order in England in the Later Middle Ages* (London: Routledge & Kegan Paul; Toronto: University of Toronto Press, 1973), 104–14.

56. Timbal Duclaux de Martin, *Droit d'asile,* 319–20.

57. Ibid., 357.

58. Ibid., 358.

59. Ibid., 435.

60. Bracton, *Laws and Customs,* II, 383.

61. H. G. Richardson and G. O. Sayles, *The Governance of Mediaeval England from the Conquest to Magna Carta* (Edinburgh: Edinburgh University Press, 1963), 441.

62. Roger D. Groot, "The Jury of Presentment before 1215," *American Journal of Legal History* 26 (1982): 22–24.

63. Hurnard, *King's Pardon,* 15.

64. Magna Carta, c. 39, *Select Charters and Other Documents of English Constitutional History,* William Stubbs, ed., 9th ed. rev. H. W. C. Davis (Oxford: Clarendon Press, 1913), 297.

65. Réville, "Abjuratio Regni," 9–10.

66. Stubbs, *Select Charters,* 347 (c. 10); Ralph B. Pugh, *Imprisonment in Medieval England* (Cambridge: Cambridge University Press, 1968), 20–21.

67. J. C. Bellamy, *The Law of Treason in England in the Later Middle Ages* (Cambridge: Cambridge University Press, 1970), 56 n. 3.

68. 13 Edw. I, Stat. Westm. Sec., c. 35, *Statutes of the Realm,* I, 88; Pugh, *Imprisonment,* 30n.

69. Bellamy, *Laws of Treason,* 53, 65, 115, 179; G. A. Holmes, "Judgment on the Younger Despenser, 1326," *English Historical Review* 70 (1955): 261–62; C. D. Ross, "Forfeitures for Treason in the Reign of Richard II," *English Historical Review* 71 (1956): 565 n. 6; Pollock and Maitland, *English Law,* II, 518 n. 4; John Bellamy, *The Tudor Law of Treason: An Introduction* (London: Routledge & Kegan Paul, 1979), 186.

70. *Contrary Commonwealth: The Theme of Exile in Medieval and Renaissance Italy* (Berkeley, Los Angeles, and London: University of California Press, 1982).

71. A. Roger Ekirch, *Bound for America: The Transportation of British Convicts, 1718–1775* (Oxford: Clarendon Press, 1991), 1.

72. Cox, *Sanctuaries and Sanctuary Seekers,* 151.

73. Ibid., 135–36.

74. Ibid., 95–149.

75. See n. 4, above.

76. Cox, *Sanctuaries and Sanctuary Seekers,* 48–94.

77. Trenholme, *Right of Sanctuary,* 69–70.

78. James Buchanan Given, *Society and Homicide in Thirteenth-Century England* (Stanford: Stanford University Press, 1977), 207–8.

79. Trenholme, *Right of Sanctuary,* 69; Hunniset, *Medieval Coroner,* 38.

80. Trenholme, *Right of Sanctuary,* 25 n. 29.

81. *Registrum Epistolarum Johannis Peckham, Archiepiscopi Cantuariensis,* Charles Trice Martin, ed., Rolls Series 77 (1885; reprint, London: 1965), III, 995.

82. 12 Edw. I, Stat. Wallie, c. 5, *Statutes of the Realm,* I, 59.

83. 9 Edw. II, Stat. 1, Articuli Cleri, c. 10, *Statutes of the Realm,* I, 173.

84. Timbal Duclaux de Martin, *Droit d'asile,* 63–67, 89–92, 142.

85. Ibid., 210–25.

86. 50 Edw. III, c. 6, *Statutes of the Realm,* I, 398; 2 Ric. II, Stat. 2, c. 3, *Statutes of the Realm* II, 12.

87. Trenholme, *Right of Sanctuary,* 26–27.

88. Cox, *Sanctuaries and Sanctuary Seekers,* 53–54, 76, 86.

89. Isobel D. Thornley, "The Destruction of Sanctuary," *Tudor Studies,* R. W. Seton-Watson, ed. (1924; reprint, Freeport, N.Y.: Books for Libraries Press, 1969), 198–207.

90. 21 Hen. VIII, c. 2, *Statutes of the Realm* III, 284.

91. 22 Hen. VIII, c. 14, *Statutes of the Realm,* III, 332–34.

92. 25 Hen. VIII, c. 22, *Statutes of the Realm,* III, 474; Cox, *Sanctuaries and Sanctuary Seekers,* 93.

93. 32 Hen. VIII, c. 12, *Statutes of the Realm,* III, 756–58.

94. Thornley, "Destruction of Sanctuary," 197 n. 75.

95. "The History of King Richard III," *The Complete Works of St. Thomas More,* Richard S. Sylvester, ed. (New Haven and London: Yale University Press, 1963), II, 30–33.

96. Timbal Duclaux de Martin, *Droit d'asile,* 434–52.

97. Quoted by Ignatius Bau, *This Ground is Holy: Church Sanctuary and Central American Refugees* (New York and Mahwah, N.J.: Paulist Press, 1985), 91.

98. Ibid.

99. Egidio Reale, *Le Droit d'asile* (Paris: Librairie du Recueil Sirey), 40–41, 73–74;

Manuel R. García-Mora, *International Law and Asylum as a Human Right* (Washington, D.C.: Public Affairs Press, 1956), 26–27, 31–40.

100. Bau, *This Ground is Holy,* 38–74.

101. Peter H. Schuck, "The Transformation of Immigration Law," *Columbia Law Review* 84 (1984), 1, quoted by Bau, *This Ground is Holy,* 38.

102. Bau, *This Ground is Holy,* 158–83.

103. The authoritative book on the sanctuary movement for Central American refugees is Ann Crittenden, *Sanctuary: A Story of American Conscience and the Law in Collision* (New York: Weidenfeld and Nicholson, 1988); also Bau's fine book.

104. Bau, *This Ground is Holy,* 172–83; William C. Ryan, "The Historical Case for the Right of Sanctuary," *The Journal of Church and State* 29 (1987): 209–32.

CRAIG EVAN KLAFTER

The Americanization of Blackstone's *Commentaries*

IT HAS BECOME an established notion of American history that William Blackstone's *Commentaries on the Laws of England* had a significant influence on American law and legal education.[1] Daniel Boorstin has noted:

> In the first century of American independence, the *Commentaries* were not merely an approach to the study of law; for most lawyers they constituted all there was of the law. The influence of Blackstone's ideas on the framers of the Federal Constitution is well known. And many an early American lawyer might have said, with Chancellor Kent, that "he owed his reputation to the fact that, when studying law . . . he had but one book, Blackstone's *Commentaries,* but that one book he mastered."[2]

Recently, Dennis R. Nolan concurred with Boorstin, claiming that Blackstone's influence on the American bar through legal education was unfettered and significant.[3] This position, however, is in need of revision.

The leaders of the postrevolutionary American bar turned to the *Commentaries,* not so much as a treatise on law, but as a model for developing American systems of legal education. Along with methods to make the diffusion of legal knowledge easier, however, the *Commentaries* included an aristocratically biased exposition of the law, and descriptions of laws neither valid in nor suited for the United States. Americans perceived Blackstone's presentation of the common law as a tool for use by the landed gentry as aristocratic, for they did not distinguish between the aristocracy and the landed gentry. Henry Wheaton, a member of the commission that rewrote New York's property law between 1826 and 1828 and a reporter for the United States Supreme Court, explained, "In England, the continuance of the landed property in the hands of the aristocracy is the basis upon which the monarchy itself may be said to rest, but, with us, it should never be forgotten that it is partibility, the frequent division and unchecked alienation of property, that are essential to the health and vigour of our republican institutions."[4] As a result, a debate ensued among leading American lawyers concerning the influence Blackstone was to be allowed in the American legal community.

The single most important product of this debate was the publication of a highly successful Americanized edition of the *Commentaries* edited by St. George Tucker.[5] Tucker used the works of European natural law writers to question Blackstone's presentation of the law and to judge its suitability for America. As a result, St. George Tucker's edition of the *Commentaries* limited Blackstone's influence on American legal education more than has been recognized, and introduced into American legal thought the propriety of questioning laws against the standards of human reason.

After the American revolution, leading American lawyers referred to Blackstone's *Commentaries* in response to a need to repopulate rapidly the ranks of the profession. The revolution had caused a vacuum in the number of practicing attorneys. Loyalist lawyers had been forced to emigrate, and many of the remaining practitioners were attracted to government posts. At the same time legal work, particularly that concerned with debt collection and property disputes, was steadily increasing. Of the colonial systems of legal education, clerkships and self-instruction were viewed as being inadequate and attendance at the Inns of Court was no longer acceptable. Thus, the leaders of the American bar addressed themselves to developing systems of legal education better suited to fulfill postrevolutionary American needs.

They began their inquiry by referring to William Blackstone's *Commentaries on the Laws of England.* There were nearly twenty-five hundred copies of the *Commentaries* available in the American colonies prior to the Declaration of Independence, including over fifteen hundred sets of the first American edition, published in 1771. This edition was available only by subscription: eight hundred and forty-nine people, including a substantial majority of the leadership of the American bar, subscribed.[6]

The *Commentaries* were unique among literature available to Americans in that they were concerned largely with issues of legal education—issues similar to the ones being faced by the leaders of the postrevolutionary American bar. Legal education in England was also in great need of improvement. Blackstone devised his program at a time when the Inns of Court and chancery were in decline.[7] Universities offered instruction only in civil law,[8] and the English clerkship system received many of the same complaints leveled at its American counterpart.[9] Whereas the Americans were looking to design an educational system suited to their image of the future needs of America, Blackstone desired to create an educational system suited to his image of the future needs of England. Living in a time of economic and political upheaval, Blackstone, as a member of the landed gentry, sought to use his talents to ensure that political power remained in the hands of the ruling classes.

The period in which the *Commentaries* were composed was a time of increasing hostility against England's ruling elite. A previously less significant commercial and bourgeois segment of society was growing into a powerful economic force as a result of the prosperity of the eighteenth century. As a result of their new economic status, members of the commercial and bourgeois segment of society sought to increase their political power. They distrusted the patrician leadership of Parliament and sought to challenge it by opening up the political system.[10] This threat, notes John Brewer, "was an alarming development for all members of the Parliamentary classes."[11]

Blackstone's reaction to this threat was characteristic of his position as a member of one of the parliamentary classes. Although his father had been a merchant, his mother's family, the Biggs of Wiltshire, were members of the landed gentry. His education was typical of his status, having attended Charterhouse and Pembroke College, Oxford. Any further doubt about his position in society is dismissed by his election to Parliament in 1761 as a defender of country interests.[12] These interests feared the possibility that the middle classes might acquire political power. It was their belief that only men of "calm, deliberate reason—the aristocracy of talent, which happened to coincide with the owners of landed property—should govern."[13] Blackstone shared the idea that political power should remain in the hands of those who possessed property.

An early opportunity to express his view came in response to the Oxfordshire election of 1754. Whereas only freeholders had previously held the right to vote, in this election the franchise was extended to copyholders. Blackstone was retained by Sir Charles Mordaunt, M.P., a prominent supporter of country interests, to contest the legality of this extension of suffrage, in the courts. Sir Charles grew impatient with the civil suit and, as an alternative, decided to seek passage of a bill in Parliament to prevent future extensions of the right to vote. At his request, Blackstone published a treatise on the subject, intended to persuade members of Parliament to support the bill.[14] Blackstone stated the basis for his argument:

> Every member of the community . . . is entitled to a vote in electing those delegates, to whose charge is committed the disposal of his property, his liberty, and his life. And this ought to be allowed him . . . provided it be probable that such a one will give his voice freely, and without influence of any kind. But since that can hardly be expected in persons of indigent fortunes, or such as are under the dominion of others . . . all popular states have therefore been obligated to establish certain qualifications; whereby some, who are suspected to have no will of their own, are excluded from voting.[15]

The rationale expressed here was so in tune with the views of the country interests and other members of the parliamentary classes that the house passed the bill within a month.[16] This was, however, only a narrow victory. Blackstone could not ignore the increasing political power of a more radical segment of society that was threatening the ruling elite in more diverse ways.[17]

The future of England would be a time of increasing political and economic tension between the ruling classes and the increasingly powerful middle class. As a member of the elite, Blackstone feared this development. But unlike other members of the parliamentary classes, he foresaw the need to develop a tool, in addition to parliamentary action, that would be used to maintain the status quo.

The ultimate tool for Blackstone was the law, and the *Commentaries* became his principal forum for teaching the elite of England how they should use the law to safeguard their positions. The *Commentaries* were intended for the use of the elite of English society—"our gentlemen of independent estates and fortune, the most useful as well as considerable body of men in the nation."[18] It was not his aim to make all of these people practicing lawyers. Rather, by educating these men in at least "a few leading principles" of law, he sought to protect them from "inferior agents" and "gross and notorious imposition."[19] Blackstone's aim was to give the nonlawyer ruling classes of England sufficient legal training to protect their economic and political power base—their possession of property.

The legal cornerstone of the *Commentaries* is the supremacy of the right to property. Blackstone stated: "So great moreover is the regard of the law for private property, that it will not authorize the least violation of it; no, not even for the general good of the whole community."[20] By establishing the right to property as the supreme right protected by law, he developed a means by which powers based on property could not be infringed. Among these powers were all major political rights—the right to vote, to stand for Parliament, and to serve on juries.

Blackstone's rationale for this, which relied on traditional seventeenth-century doctrine, was that people who lack property can too easily be bought and thus "have no will of their own."[21] Hence Blackstone employed a near perfect means by which the elite could fend off political encroachment from the middle class. The elite faced two challenges—to limit the franchise to freehold property holders and to maintain their freehold property interests. So long as they succeeded, their political survival was ensured. Blackstone's gift to his elite brethren was to show them how the land could be used to accomplish this end.

His problem was how to transform the law, which had always been a difficult discipline to study, into a subject that educated nonlawyers could easily learn. Blackstone's interest in addressing this problem is explained in his preface to the *Analysis of the Laws of England,* which according to John M. Finnis was intended to be "an exact outline or abstract of the *Commentaries.*"[22] Blackstone wrote that his goal in the *Commentaries* was "to mark out a plan of the laws of England, so comprehensive as that every title might be reduced under some or another of its general heads, which the student might afterwards pursue to any degree of minuteness; and at the same time so contracted, that the gentleman might with tolerable application contemplate and understand the whole."[23] Blackstone sought to make the *Commentaries* into a textbook for instruction and a treatise for reference.

Blackstone's method on undertaking this task was modeled on that of Jean Jacques Burlamaqui in his *The Principles of Natural and Political Law.*[24] Burlamaqui emphasized the importance of uncovering the fundamental principles that lay beneath the legal system and then categorizing the law in accordance with those principles.

Blackstone modified this approach by presenting law as deserving unquestioning aesthetic reverence. He was concerned that people would come to feel that anyone might understand all the criteria of law and would conclude that law could be tested by the standards of human reason. Daniel Boorstin explained: "A sublime and incomprehensible natural grandeur was found in the disorder, complexity, and even in the obscurity of the law. Man was discouraged from any attempt to improve the law because the English system contained latent, undiscoverable perfections which he might unwittingly destroy. The aesthetic appeal of the laws of

England, although to some extent rationally explained in the *Commentaries*, itself seemed a cause for limiting the scope of man's destructive reason."[25] For example, in Blackstone's explanation of fundamental principles, he always emphasized the close relationship of English laws to the laws of nature, suggesting that English law had the aesthetic virtues of nature.[26]

Blackstone utilized this approach in his description of property law. He began by stating that the right to possess property originated in Genesis, where God gave man "dominion over all the earth."[27] Pursuant to this, an individual in the state of nature acquired a right to property as long as he used it (e.g., a man resting in the shade of a tree had the right not to be ejected from that spot). "But when mankind increased in number, craft, and ambition," wrote Blackstone, "it became necessary to entertain conceptions of more permanent dominion."[28]

After explaining the development of this need by rendering a detailed legal history of the feudal system, Blackstone then proceeded to present eighteenth-century property law categorized according to the various forms of property (e.g., freehold, joint tenancy) and according to how an individual obtained legal title to property (e.g., purchase, occupancy). The end result was to transform English property law, which long had been presented as a hodgepodge of details and procedures, into an elegant science through systematization based on principles.

Blackstone applied this technique to all aspects of the English legal system and through his *Commentaries* used it to present the law in a manner that could be easily understood and referred to, while placing laws out of the reach of destructive reasoning. Although the *Commentaries* had been designed to benefit the landed interest, their easily accessible presentation of the law was well suited to the American situation. But just as this intellectual invasion was gaining momentum, the American legal profession was faced with a dilemma.

The American revolution was viewed by the colonists in part as a struggle to regain lost English legal rights. Yet years of war against perceived unreasonable parliamentary action caused people to question the desirability of adopting the English legal system. The focal point for this dilemma among legal scholars was Blackstone's *Commentaries*, which threatened to entrench the English legal system, without qualification, into the new United States. Some lauded Blackstone's simplified method of presentation and clear organization. Others welcomed the scholarly contribution of the *Commentaries* while expressing concern about its aristocratically biased legal philosophy. And yet others were so fearful of the unchecked adoption of Blackstone's anti-Republican presentation of the English legal system that they sought to prevent the *Commentaries* from influencing American law. Battle lines in this debates were drawn along political party lines.

Staunch Federalists, most notably Tapping Reeve and Peter Van Schaack, embraced Blackstone's work.[29] No doubt they found a need technically to modify points of law that were out of step with American decisions. They did not regard Blackstone's bias particularly bothersome, however; nor did they find a need to object to American law students' ferocious appetites for the *Commentaries*.

Moderate Federalists, such as James Wilson and Zephaniah Swift, however, exhibited reservations about the text. Wilson cautioned readers:

> As I have mentioned Sir William Blackstone, let me speak of him explicitly as it becomes me. I cannot consider him a zealous friend of republicanism. One of his survivors or successors in office, has characterized him by the appellation of an anti-republican lawyer. On the subject of government, I think I can plainly discover his jealousies and attachments. . . . As author of the *Commentaries* he possesses uncommon merit. . . . In public law, however, he should be consulted with a cautious prudence. . . . On every account, therefore, he should be read and studied. He deserves to be much admired; but he ought not to be implicitly followed.[30]

Although Wilson was troubled by Blackstone's anti-Republican leanings, he still found much about the *Commentaries* to admire and recommend—in particular, its exposition of the law as it applied to English conditions, much of which was still applicable to American conditions.

Swift's hesitation about the *Commentaries* was evident in his *A System of Laws of the State of Connecticut*. This work flattered Blackstone by applying his method and organization to American law while purposefully excluding his antirepublican bias. Indeed, unlike Blackstone, who geared his writings to the elite of English society, Swift dedicated his work to "a more general diffusion of knowledge among all classes of people."[31] He intended this work to replace the *Commentaries* within Connecticut.

These moderate Federalists were sufficiently concerned about the *Commentaries* to take modest actions to prevent its unquestioned influence on American law. Some Republican lawyers, however, believed that much more drastic action was required. Republican lawyers such as St.

George Tucker and Thomas Jefferson spearheaded a campaign to drastically limit Blackstone's influence in America. They advocated the exclusion of the text from American legal education because they thought the presentation too superficial and the substantive bias too persuasive. Tucker complained: "the student who had read the *Commentaries* . . . was lead [*sic*] to believe that he was a thorough proficient in the law. . . . This sudden revolution in the course of study may be considered as having produced effects almost as pernicious as the want of a regular and systematic guide, since it cannot be doubted that it has contributed to usher into the profession a great number, whose superficial knowledge of the law has been almost as soon forgotten, as acquired."[32]

Jefferson wrote to Horatio G. Spafford: "I join in your reprobation of our . . . lawyers for their adherence to England and monarchy, in preference to their own country and its constitution. . . . I ascribe much of this to the substitution of Blackstone for my Lord Coke, as an elementary work."[33] As Republicans read it, the *Commentaries* were not suited to the education of the first generation of American lawyers.

The task of preventing the use of Blackstone proved most difficult. Tucker's concern could be dealt with by supplementing the *Commentaries* with additional reading or forms of instruction. Jefferson's concern could be too easily dismissed by Federalists as being based upon partisan politics. In their search for alternative means of discounting Blackstonian influence, Republicans found a champion in Charles-Louis de Secondat, Baron de la Brede et de Montesquieu.

Montesquieu's *De L'Esprit des Lois* [The Spirit of the Laws] was implanted into the American legal tradition during the period between 1760 and 1802. Paul Spurlin has noted that in colonial newspapers between 1760 and 1776, "in actual inches quoted, when sources were named, Montesquieu surpassed Locke and compared favorably with Blackstone."[34] Between 1762 and 1797, a steady flow of foreign editions of *The Spirit of Laws* entered America, as is indicated by numerous American newspaper advertisements offering their sale.[35] Many of the educational leaders of the postrevolutionary American bar obtained copies of the text during this period.[36] More importantly, the work had so great an impact on these leaders that they recommended it as required reading to law students.[37] By the time the first American edition of *The Spirit of Laws* was published in 1802, Montesquieu had become a leading authority for American jurisprudence.[38]

Although *The Spirit of Laws* was most widely read for its pronouncements on the structure of government, lawyers also found in it much insight into issues of legal education. Montesquieu's particular contribution concerned how much of the English legal tradition should be relied upon in creating the American legal system. By setting out to discover the fundamental principles on which the law was based, Montesquieu argued that the law is inherently tied to the physical environments from which it arises. Since the physical environment of America was different from that of England, Montesquieu was employed to argue that English law must first be Americanized, where necessary, before it could be adopted into American law.

Montesquieu began his inquiry, as did Blackstone, by showing that laws are based upon fundamental principles: "I have laid down the first principles, and have found that the particular cases follow naturally from them; that the histories of all nations are only consequences of them; and that every particular law is connected with another law, or depends on some other of a more general extent."[39] Blackstone delved into legal principles in order to argue the supremacy of property rights and in order to systematize the law so that it could be more easily taught. Montesquieu, however, resorted to first principles as a means for discovering the character of society.

Montesquieu called this the "general spirit of mankind." He described it as being a societal soul formed by the influences of climate, religion, laws, government, precedents, morals, and customs. The variation of these influences from society to society results in each having a unique soul. The unique soul in turn permeated a society's institutions and affects its interactions. An understanding of this, according to Montesquieu, is essential to any societal leader, since the introduction of a change in one institution must be consistent with the societal soul and may affect other institutions.[40]

The importance of this philosophy to the question of the acceptance of foreign laws into a society was explained by Montesquieu as he described the role of positive laws:

> They should be adapted in such a manner to the people for whom they are made, as to render it very unlikely for those of one nation to be proper for another.
>
> They should be relative to the nature and principle of the actual, or in-

> tended, government; whether they form this principle, as in the case of political laws, or whether they support it, as may be said of civil institutions.
>
> They should be relative to the climate, whether hot or cold, of each country, to the quality of the soil, to its situation and bigness, to the manner of living of the natives, whether husbandmen, huntsmen, or shepherds; they should have a relation to the degree of liberty which the constitution will bear; to the religion of the inhabitants, to their inclinations, riches, number, commerce, manners, and customs. In fine they have relations amongst themselves, as also with their origin, with the object of the legislator, and with the order of things on which they are established, in all with different lights they ought to be considered.[41]

Montesquieu argued here that the requirements of nature are different in every society. Since laws must be made in conformity to the requirements of nature, laws can be made only to apply to a given society. While there is an obvious tension between Montesquieu's relativism and the notion of inalienable rights, they were not deemed mutually exclusive. Inalienable rights were universal rights, which political institutions were designed to secure, while laws were the instruments these institutions used to accomplish this end. Laws could vary from country to country, depending on local circumstances, and still maintain the goal of securing the same inalienable right.

For example, two countries could recognize the right not to be discriminated against on the basis of race. One country, with a multiracial population and a history of discrimination, may consider it necessary to establish affirmative action laws. Whereas another country, with a racially homogeneous population and no history of discrimination, now faced with an immigration of members of another race, may consider it sufficient to establish a law that prohibits racial discrimination without establishing a system of quotas. Both the concepts of relativism and inalienable rights exist without conflict.

By introducing Montesquieu's philosophy into the debate over the unqualified acceptance of the *Commentaries* into American law, opponents of Blackstone found an ally to help temper the influence of English law. According to Gilbert Chinard, Thomas Jefferson was one of the first American lawyers to espouse Montesquieu's views: "Everywhere in *The Spirit of Laws*, he found illustrations of the theory which he maintained all his life that laws and constitutions are variable and changing and must be altered in accordance with climate, local conditions, and new circumstances. He even went one step further than Montesquieu in his relativism, when he proclaimed that a generation has no right to bind by laws the following generation."[42] Jefferson relied on this philosophy in revising the laws of the state of Virginia.

Between 1776 and 1780, Jefferson played a key role in introducing a series of legal reforms to the Virginia legislature designed to prevent English law as presented by Blackstone from establishing itself in Virginian jurisprudence. As the leading member of the Committee of Revisors Appointed by the General Assembly of Virginia, he was largely responsible for introducing one hundred twenty-six bills that served to revise the common law, criminal law, the law of descents, laws concerning religious freedom, laws concerning public education, the statute laws of Virginia, and English statutes. Within ten years, due to the additional efforts of James Madison, almost all these bills were enacted into law. Jefferson had succeeded in politically limiting the influence of the *Commentaries* on Virginia law.[43]

St. George Tucker, however, was still apprehansive about Blackstone's influence. Tucker's concerns were threefold: (1) in spite of the revision of the laws of Virginia, most lawyers and judges would still rely on the *Commentaries* because they lacked access to the revised laws[44]; (2) the anti-Republican influence of Blackstone still threatened other states and the federal government; and (3) law students would be seduced by the *Commentaries* before having the opportunity to learn of its faults.[45] By 1790, Tucker realized that Blackstone was too firmly established in America to be effectively banned.[46] He still believed, however, that Blackstone's influence could be curtailed.[47]

Tucker set out via American legal education to limit the *Commentaries'* influence on lawyers and the judiciary. He began as Professor of Law and Police at the College of William and Mary in 1790. He assigned *The Spirit of Laws* and quoted extensively from it in his lectures, with the aim of using Montesquieu's relativism to justify questioning the applicability of English law, as described by Blackstone, to America.[48] Tucker then utilized the writings of European philosophes—including, in order of degree of use, Montesquieu, John Locke, Emmerich von Vattel, Jean-Jacques Rousseau, Matthew Bacon, Thomas Paine, Francis Hutcheson, Jean-Jacques Burlamaqui, James Burgh, Baron Samuel von Pufendorf, and Hugo Grotius. He wanted to show that reason should be the ultimate test in determining the soundness of the law and its application. As the decade progressed, Tucker sought to reach a wider audience through the publication of his own edition of the *Commentaries,* which offered a step-by-step guide to Blackstone's limitations.

St. George Tucker's edition of the *Commentaries* was designed primarily to show where and why Blackstone's presentation of English law was not properly suited to American society. He wrote, "as the common law is a collection of general customs, it may not be amiss to inquire whether particular customs have any, or what force, among us!"[49] He achieved this by adding footnotes to the text, where laws and legal concepts did not apply to America, directing the reader to an editor's appendix that included a series of essays. These essays can be grouped into three parts: those that concern dispelling Blackstone's anti-Republican bias, those that concern the reception of the common law into America, and those that concern how English law had been revised by American law or question the soundness and applicability to the United States of English law yet to be revised. In all, Tucker showed, contrary to the teachings of Blackstone, that the law could and should be questioned.

St. George Tucker began his inquiry by disputing Blackstone's anti-Republican bias. This bias, according to Tucker, was rooted in the proposition that sovereign power resides wherever laws are made.[50] In England, this meant that sovereignty lay with Parliament and that the only people who should have access to that power were members of the parliamentary classes.[51] Against this view, Tucker argued that sovereignty should lie with the people. Relying on Rousseau and James Burgh, he wrote that the right of making laws can be acquired only by the consent of the people.[52] This consent is given when people enter into written compacts designed, citing Thomas Paine, to authorize government to enact and enforce only specific types of laws.[53]

In the United States, these written compacts initially took the form of state constitutions. Later the states agreed to relinquish some of their authority to a federal government. The federal constitution, which ensued, was a written compact between the states and the federal government authorized by the people. Hence, the people granted limited powers to the states, which the states in turn, with the consent of the people, divided with the federal government. The people were the ultimate power-granting authority. But according to Tucker, the power to grant authority to govern is only part of sovereign power.[54]

Sovereign power also requires the ability to make sure that government does not overstep its authority. In the United States, this power was retained by the people and the states as representatives of the people. Tucker declared:

> But to guard against encroachments on the powers of the several states, in their politic character, and of the people, both in their individual and sovereign capacity, an amendatory article was added, immediately after the government was organized, declaring; that the powers not delegated to the United States, by the constitution, nor prohibited by it to the states, are reserved to the states, respectively, or to the people. And, still further, to guard the people against constructive usurpations and encroachments on their rights, another article declares; that the enumeration of certain rights in the constitution, shall not be construed to deny, or disparage, others retained by the people. The sum of all which appears to be, that the powers delegated to the federal government are, in all cases, to receive the most strict construction that the instrument will bear, where the rights of a state or of the people, either collectively or individually, may be drawn in question.[55]

These amendments were not, in Tucker's view, the only means for ensuring that powers retained by the people and the states were not usurped by the federal government. Tucker wrote:

> If it be asked, what would be the consequences in case the federal government should exercise powers not warranted by the constitution, the answer seems to be, that where the act of usurpation may immediately affect an individual, the remedy is to be sought by recourse to that judiciary, to which the cognisance of the case properly belongs. Where it may affect a state, the state legislature, whose rights will be invaded by every such act, will be ready to mark the innovation and sound the alarm to the people: and thereby either effect a change in the federal representation, or procure in the mode prescribed by the constitution, further "declaratory and restrictive clauses," by way of amendment thereto.[56]

If the government should ever grossly abuse its power, Tucker argued, referring to Francis Hutcheson and quoting from the Declaration of Independence, the people would be freed from the obligations of their compact and could insist upon a new form of government.[57] In this way, governments depend "upon the nature and extent of those powers which the people have reserved to themselves, as the Sovereign; or rather, upon the extent of those, which they have delegated to the government; or, which the government in the course of its administration may have usurped."[58] Thus, sovereignty does not rest with those who make laws; it rests with those who authorized government to make laws and who can limit and even retract governmental power—the people.

Having both highlighted and dispelled Blackstone's anti-Republican bias, Tucker turned his attention to the reception of English law in America. Blackstone wrote of this issue, noting that the colonies are of two types: those deserted and uncultivated by right of occupancy and those peopled and cultivated as claimed by conquest or ceded by treaty. English people who colonized by right of occupancy took with them aspects of the English law that were suited to their new situations. In conquered or ceded territories with prior laws of their own, the law at the time of acquisition remained in effect until changed by the king. Blackstone ascribed America to this latter group, stating that it was obtained either by conquest or by treaties. Thus, he argued that Americans had no right to claim the common law and were instead subject to the laws previously in existence and the control of Parliament.[59]

Tucker contested this, claiming that the British who colonized America brought with them the rights and privileges of Englishmen. He noted, citing Pufendorf and Grotius, that a justly conquered or ceded nation must submit to the government of the conquerors or of those to whom they have been ceded.[60] Moreover, he wrote, quoting Grotius, that "when a people, by one consent, go to form colonies, it is the original of a new and independent people; for they are not sent out to be slaves, but to enjoy equal privileges and freedom."[61] The British who settled America conquered it, with the exception of New York and New Jersey, which were ceded to England by the Treaty of Breda in 1667, and brought with them that portion of English law that they considered necessary to maintain their rights.

The colonists, finding themselves in a new country, remote from England, needed municipal laws and the right to adapt them to their circumstances. "The municipal laws of the parent state," wrote Tucker, "being better known to them, than those of any other nation, a recurrence to them would naturally be had, for that decisions of all questions of right and wrong, which should arise among them, until leisure and experience should enable them to make laws better adapted to their own peculiar situation."[62] He argued that only the colonists could have judged the applicability of English law to local circumstances and cited the crown's granting to the colonies of legislatures of their own, as proof.

Colonial legislatures took immediate action, according to Tucker, to modify the common law to fit their own domestic concerns. Massachusetts changed inheritance laws, which had favored the eldest son so that they distributed the estate to all the immediate family. Rhode Island and Pennsylvania adopted laws that fostered religious freedom. In Virginia, laws were passed for relief of creditors against fraudulent devices. By the eve of the American revolution, Tucker argued, each colony had developed its own body of laws.[63]

Tucker thus turned his attention to the effect of the revolution on the reception of English law. He argued that the common and statutory laws of England, founded on monarchical government and inconsistent with democratic principles, were annulled in each state by the establishment of democratic governments. In addition, all other parts of English law that had not been brought into use by colonial governments were made obsolete and incapable of revival, except by constitutional or legislative authority. On the other hand, all laws in use prior to the revolution, not falling into the above categories, even if they were repugnant to the common law, were unquestionably established. State constitutions, noted Tucker, confirmed the existence and authority of the common law and statutes in use at the time of their ratification and also authorized future changes by state legislatures.[64]

In describing the impact of the revolution on English law, Tucker pointed out that the impact was manifested differently from state to state. He noted that when the American states declared themselves independent of the crown, each state from that moment became sovereign and independent of Great Britain and all other powers. Each state had its own constitution and laws; there was no common law among them, only the law of nations. He wrote: "From hence it follows, that the adoption of the common law, or statutes of England, in one state, or several, or even in all, although it might produce a general conformity, in their municipal codes, yet as such adoption was the separate act of each state, it could not operate so as to give to those laws a sanction superior to any other laws of the states, respectively; inasmuch as each state would still have retained the power of changing, or rejecting them, whenever it should think proper."[65] Thus, Tucker argued that as a result of the revolution, there was no such thing as a national common or municipal law.

The remaining issue Tucker addressed was the effect the United States Constitution had on the reception of English law in America.

Tucker began by pointing out that in establishing the federal government, the intention was, as confirmed by the Tenth Amendment, to give it only limited powers. He explained, referring to Vattel, that the Tenth Amendment is nothing more than "an express recognition of the law of nations," which permits independent states to unite in a confederacy. Although the states may voluntarily permit the federal government to exercise some of their sovereign powers, they will still retain their independent sovereignty.[66] In addition, he argued, quoting Matthew Bacon, that the powers given to the federal government, in order to be consistent with maintaining independent state sovereignty, must be strictly interpreted.[67]

Tucker then examined all the "enumerated" powers in the Constitution and concluded that there was no grant of general jurisdiction to either federal or state courts in cases at common law. Nevertheless, he discussed the claim that this jurisdiction might have been granted by implication. He presented five arguments in opposition to this view. First, the Tenth Amendment bars such a construction. Second, it would be absurd to grant to the federal government power to revive parts of English law that state constitutions had rejected. Third, such a construction abridging the rights of sovereign states by implication could be used as a precedent to virtually annihilate the states. Fourth, numerous provisions of state constitutions, which mandated changes in the common law and authorized legislatures to modify the law, would be nullified. Fifth, references to the common law, to common law rights, or to common law courts in the United States Constitution refer to the laws of the several states rather than the laws of the federal government. Tucker argued that federal courts could assume jurisdiction only over cases where jurisdiction was expressly granted by the Constitution.[68]

In all, Tucker concluded that the only English laws validly received into America originated from the period before the revolution—a period when Blackstone's *Commentaries* had had little impact. As Tucker portrayed events, the only influence Blackstone's work was entitled to in post-revolutionary America was to explain that portion of the common law in use prior to the American revolution that had not been modified or nullified by the revolution, by state constitutions, or by state legislative action. Tucker was, in effect, cautioning his readers not to view the *Commentaries* as a statement of American common law—a power reserved to state legislatures and courts by state constitutions. What remained for Tucker to explain was which aspects of English law, as portrayed by Blackstone, had been changed in America or required revision because of their questionable soundness and applicability to the United States.

Tucker discussed many example of laws that had undergone, or would undergo, such revisions. For example, he examined the law of expatriation, which was in need of new interpretation in order to allow Americans to free themselves from allegiance to the crown. Pursuing his political objections to Blackstone's elitism based on property ownership, he also devoted a substantial portion of his discussion to American property law.

The right of expatriation was central to Americans' claims of independence. If it did not exist, the majority of the population of America could not claim United States citizenship. Blackstone opposed the right of expatriation, writing, "it is a principle of universal law, that the natural born subject of one prince cannot by any act of his own, no, not by swearing allegiance to another, put off, or discharge his natural allegiance to the former."[69]

Tucker countered this position on the grounds that there was nothing in divine law, natural law, or the law of nations to support Blackstone's statement. He showed that expatriation was not prohibited by divine law, noting that the Old Testament records that the Israelites were expatriated from Egypt by the hand of Jehovah Himself. He argued that the law of nature did not prohibit expatriation, since in nature all men were equal and thus not subject to the control of princes. And he deferred to the conclusions of Vattel, Grotius, Burlamaqui, and Pufendorf, noting that the law of nations prescribed that "every man hath a natural right to migrate from one state to another."[70] In spite of all this, however, Tucker still found the need to refer to the philosophical writings of John Locke in order to show that reason alone could disprove Blackstone's claim.[71]

Locke argued, according to Tucker, that those who believed expatriation to be illegal based it on the notion that a father who swore allegiance to a prince bound his posterity as well through the inheritance of his property. This notion was considered unsound "for his son, when a man, being altogether as free as the father, any act of the father can no more give away the liberty of the son, than it can of any body else."[72] The son, upon coming of age, would be free to give up his father's property and thus free to emigrate. Tucker implied that all the arguments above were the basis for a Virginia act, and Pennsylvania and Vermont constitutional declarations, which confirmed an individual's right to emigrate.[73]

Tucker reserved his greatest attention for property law. "The almost total change in the system of laws relative to property, both real and personal, in Virginia," wrote Tucker, "appeared more particularly to demand a strict scrutiny, and investigation."[74] His treatment of the law of descents and the modes of acquiring unoccupied or waste and unappropriated lands is representative. Of all the areas of property law, Blackstone said that "the doctrine of descents, or the law of inheritances in fee-simple, is a point of the highest importance; and is indeed the principal object of the laws of real property in England."[75] It was deserving of this position because it virtually ensured the elite's right to property and to the political power linked to property ownership.

After the revolution, however, the law was changed in America to make it more compatible with democratic ideals. One of the first steps taken in Virginia was the passage of an act declaring that the tenants of real property by estate in tail would thereafter hold the same in fee simple, thus giving them the right and freedom to sell or transfer their land. In 1785 the Virginia legislature rewrote the whole body of the law of descents.[76]

Tucker described these changes, showing step-by-step how the new rules were directly contrary to the common law as expressed by Blackstone. Under the new law, land could be inherited only by fee simple, whereas the common law had allowed land to be offered for inheritance with numerous restrictions. The estate of a person who died intestate, which had been guaranteed to the eldest son (not including bastards) according to the common law, would go to all his children equally—including bastards. Where two equal claimants to an estate existed, the common law would give any real property to both in joint tenancy, thus preserving the whole of the land for future generations. Virginia statute mandated that such property be transferred as tenancy in common, thus permitting either recipient to sell or transfer a share. Where the common law had permitted property to be held until a beneficiary was born, Virginia required that the beneficiary should already be alive. In all, Tucker showed that the new statute had made Blackstone's essay on descents useless in Virginia.[77]

The mode of acquiring unoccupied or waste and unappropriated lands was of little importance to Blackstone. England had no waste and unappropriated lands. According to the *Commentaries,* title by occupancy was "confined by the laws of England within a very narrow compass; and was extended only to a single instance."[78] In a country as vast and undeveloped as the United States, laws favoring occupancy and development of waste and unappropriated lands were desirable.

Tucker explained that, prior to the revolution, waste and undeveloped lands could be acquired only by royal grant, by vote of the general assembly, or by grant of the governor. But, in 1779, the Virginia legislature passed an act that completely revamped the mode of acquiring these lands. This act did more than just modify English law; it introduced into Virginia entirely new laws exclusively suited to the needs of a frontier society. It instituted the notion of adverse possession—a method of acquisition of title to real property by mere possession for a statutory period and under certain conditions. It permitted any person to acquire title to any amount of waste and unappropriated lands desired (excluding certain areas), by paying two dollars to the commonwealth. It also authorized any person to acquire title to land forfeited or escheated to the state, by paying twenty-five pounds per hundred acres. Pursuant to this act, any citizen of Virginia could obtain fee-simple title to land, which would not have been possible in Blackstone's England.[79]

Tucker had demonstrated that considerable caution was required in the use of Blackstone's *Commentaries* as a reference by American lawyers. His treatise served to highlight and clarify the anti-Republican bias of the *Commentaries.* He also demonstrated that, although Blackstone might be of use as a reference for the application of the common law as it existed prior to the revolution, the *Commentaries* not only did not cover aspects of the new and developing American laws, but indeed often opposed the very foundations of such laws.

As American politics shifted at the beginning of the nineteenth century, the American bar grew to appreciate Tucker's concerns about Blackstone. Tucker had sought the publication of his work as early as 1794. But the Philadelphia publishing community did not perceive sufficient demand to merit publication until 1801. During this six-year period, James Wilson and Zephaniah Swift had been sent copies of Tucker's manuscript. They were won over by the work, and strongly encouraged its publication. When St. George Tucker's *Blackstone's Commentaries with Notes of Reference, to the Constitution and Laws, of the Federal Government of the United States; and of the Commonwealth of Virginia* was finally published in Philadelphia by William Young Birch and Abraham Small in 1803, it was an instant success.[80]

While detailed sales records for Tucker's *Blackstone* have not survived, communications between Tucker and his publisher provide some insight into the number of books sold. On April 7, 1802, Abraham Small wrote to Tucker, stating that his firm planned three printings of the work in the amounts of 2500, 1500, and 100 copies respectively.[81] According to the terms of the publication agreement, Birch and Small would pay royalties at the rate of $2.50 per copy up to 1,000 copies or $4,000 for their entire copyright.[82] By February 22, 1803, two and a half months prior to publication, the number of subscribers was so great that Birch and Small decided to pay Tucker $4,000 for the right to publish all 5,000 copies of the work.[83] It appears that all copies of the first edition were sold, for on February 13, 1818, Small wrote to tell Tucker of his intention to publish a second edition.[84] To put these numbers in perspective, the first American printing of Blackstone's *Commentaries* in 1771 had sales of 849 copies. It has been estimated that there were 2,500 copies of the *Commentaries* in use in the colonies by 1775.[85]

St. George Tucker's work became the definitive edition of Blackstone available in America until 1852, when John L. Wendell published his edition. Charles T. Cullen noted: "Until the introduction of the case method of teaching law in the late nineteenth century commentaries and treatises were actually the only texts or references students and lawyers had for studying American law, and St. George Tucker's *Blackstone* was the only summary of similar dimensions available until Chancellor James Kent of New York began publishing his *Commentaries on American Law* in 1826."[86]

Elizabeth Bauer found that Tucker's *Commentaries* acquired popularity with the United States Supreme Court.[87] In addition, Alfred Reed claimed that Tucker's work "fixed the Blackstone Tradition in this country."[88] Unfortunately, Reed had not realized that Tucker had fixed a severely limited and altered Blackstone tradition in America.

Tucker's greatest influence on this tradition was to bring the law down from the high altar on which it had been placed by Blackstone. He used Montesquieu's relativism to establish the appropriateness of questioning the law, and the works of European natural law writers to show that reason should be the law's ultimate test. He described the state and federal constitutions as the people's primary means of redacting reason into a defense against unreasonable laws and the unreasonable application of laws. In all, Tucker introduced a method of viewing the law, which, presented in a work that became the standard text for a generation of lawyers, separated American legal thought from Blackstone and the English legal system.

NOTES

1. William Blackstone, *Commentaries on the Laws of England* (Oxford: Clarendon Press, 1765).

2. Daniel J. Boorstin, *The Mysterious Science of the Law* (Cambridge: Harvard University Press, 1941), 3. See also Daniel J. Boorstin, *The Americans: The Colonial Experience* (New York: Vintage Books, 1958), 202.

3. Dennis R. Nolan, "Sir William Blackstone and the New American Republic: A Study of Intellectual Impact," 51 *New York University Law Review* 731 (1976).

4. Quoted in Peggy A. Rabin, *Fathers to Daughters: The Legal Foundations of Female Emancipation* (Westport, Conn.: Greenwood Press, 1980), 66.

5. St. George Tucker, *Blackstone's Commentaries with Notes of Reference, to the Constitution and Laws, of the Federal Government of the United States; and of the Commonwealth of Virginia,* 5 vols. (Philadelphia: William Young Birch and Abraham Small, 1803).

6. James Bradley Thayer, "The Teaching of English Law at Universities," 9 *Harvard Law Review* 169, 170 (1895); Sir William Blackstone, *Commentaries on the Laws of England,* 4 vols. (Philadelphia: Robert Bell, 1771–72), 4: "Names of the Subscribers."

7. William Blackstone, *Commentaries on the Laws of England,* 4 vols. (1765; reprint ed., Chicago: University of Chicago Press, 1979), I: 25.

8. Ibid., 3.

9. Ibid., 31; Harry Kirk, *Portrait of a Profession* (London: Oyez Publishing, 1976), 48.

10. H. T. Dickinson, *Liberty and Property: Political Ideology in Eighteenth Century Britain* (London: Methuen, 1977), 195.

11. John Brewer, *Party Ideology and Popular Politics at the Accession of George III* (Cambridge: Cambridge University Press, 1981), 267.

12. Stanley N. Katz, "Introduction," in Blackstone, *Commentaries* (1765; reprint ed., Chicago: University of Chicago Press, 1979), I:iii-iv.

13. Dickinson, *Liberty and Property,* 165.

14. R. J. Robson, *The Oxfordshire Election of 1754: A Study in the Interplay of City, County and University Politics* (Oxford: Oxford University Press, 1949), 144–46; Lewis C. Warden, *The Life of Blackstone* (Charlottesville, VA.: Michie Co., 1938), 132–33; William Blackstone, *Considerations on the Question, Whether Tenants . . . Are Freeholders Qualified to Vote in Elections for Knights of the Shire* (London: Printed for R. Baldwin, 1763).

15. William Blackstone, *Law Tracts,* 2 vols. (Oxford: Clarendon Press, 1762), I:106.

16. Warden, *Life of Blackstone,* 132–33.

17. Dickinson, *Liberty and Property,* 195.

18. Blackstone, *Commentaries,* I:7.

19. Ibid.

20. Ibid., 135.

21. Ibid., 165.

22. William Blackstone, *An Analysis of the Laws of England,* 6th rev. ed. (Oxford: Clarendon Press, 1771); John M. Finnis, "Blackstone's Theoretical Intentions," 12 *National Law Forum* 163, 164 (1967).

23. Blackstone, *An Analysis of the Laws of England,* iv.

24. Jean-Jacques Burlamaqui, *The Principles of Natural and Political Law* (Geneva: Chez Barrillot & Fils, 1747); Paul Lucas, "Ex parte Sir William Blackstone, 'Plagiarist': A Note on Blackstone and the Natural Law," 7 *American Journal of Legal History* 147 (1963).

25. Boorstin, *Mysterious Science,* 105.

26. Ibid., 85–105.

27. Blackstone, *Commentaries,* II:2.

28. Ibid., 4.

29. Nolan, "William Blackstone," 762.

30. James Wilson, *The Works of the Honourable James Wilson, LL.D.,* Bird Wilson, ed., 2 vols. (Philadelphia: Lorenzo Press, 1804), I: 21–22.

31. Zephaniah Swift, *A System of the Laws of the State of Connecticut,* 2 vols. (Windham, Conn.: John Byrne, 1795), I:4.

32. Tucker, *Blackstone's Commentaries,* I: iv.

33. Thomas Jefferson, *The Writings of Thomas Jefferson,* H. A. Washington, ed., 9 vols. (Washington, D.C.: Taylor and Maury, 1853–54), VI: 334, quoted in Julian S. Waterman, "Thomas Jefferson and Blackstone's *Commentaries,*" 27 *Illinois Law Review* 629, at 637 n. 49 (1932–33).

34. Charles-Louis de Secondat, Baron de la Bede et de Montesquieu, *De L'Esprit des Lois* [The Spirit of the Laws] (Geneva: Barrillot, 1748); Paul Merrill Spurlin, *Montesquieu in America, 1760–1801* (New York: Octagon Books, 1969), 157.

35. *Maryland Gazette,* August 26, 1762; *Boston Gazette,* September 23–October 7, 1771, and March 29–August 9, 1784; *General Advertiser* (Philadelphia), June 28–September 1, 1791, and May 8–May 18, 1793; *Aurora General Advertiser* (Philadelphia), August 14–November 6, 1797.

36. Paul Merrill Spurlin, *The French Enlightenment in America* (Athens: University of Georgia Press, 1984), 88–89; Albert J. Harno, *Legal Education in the United States* (1953: reprint ed., Westport, Conn.: Greenwood Press, 1980), 22. Specific references to key individuals are as follows: James Wilson—Francis Jean de Chastellux, *Voyages de M. le Marquis de Chastellux dans l'Amérique septentrionale dans les années 1780, 1781, & 1782,* 2 vols. (Paris: Prault, 1786), I:185–86; Peter Van Schaack to Henry Walton, June 3, 1788, in Henry C. Van Schaack, *The Life of Peter Van Schaack, LL.D.* (New York: D. Appleton & Co., 1842), 54; James Kent, *Commentaries on American Law,* 4 vols. (1826; reprint ed., New York: Da Capo Press, 1971), I: 1; Thomas Jefferson—Gilbert Chinard, *The Commonplace Book of Thomas Jefferson* (Baltimore: Johns Hopkins University Press, 1926); St. George Tucker, *Blackstone's Commentaries,* I: Editor's Appendix, 43.

37. Spurlin, *Montesquieu,* 259; Simon E. Baldwin, "The Study of Elementary Law, the Proper Beginning of a Legal Education," 13 *Yale Law Journal,* 1 (1903).

38. Montesquieu, *The Spirit of Laws,* trans. Thomas Nugent, 5th ed. (1773; reprint ed., Worcester, Mass.: Isaiah Thomas, Jr., 1802).

39. Montesquieu, *The Spirit of Laws,* trans. Thomas Nugent, David Wallace Carrithers, ed. (1750; reprint ed., Berkeley: University of California Press, 1977), 91.

40. Ibid., 289–97.

41. Ibid., 104–105.

42. Chinard, *Commonplace Book,* 38.

43. Dumas Malone, *Jefferson the Virginian* (Boston: Little, Brown and Company, 1948), 261–63.

44. Tucker, *Blackstone's Commentaries,* I: xii.

45. Ibid., iv

46. Ibid., v.

47. Ibid., xviii.

48. Charles T. Cullen, *St. George Tucker and the Law in Virginia, 1772–1804* (New York: Garland Publishing, 1987), 145, 205.

49. Tucker, *Blackstone's Commentaries,* I:ix.

50. Ibid., 48.

51. Dickinson, *Liberty and Property,* 165; Blackstone, *Law Tracts,* I: 106.

52. Tucker, *Blackstone's Commentaries,* I: Editor's Appendix, 8, 9.

53. Ibid., 9.

54. Ibid., 142–46.

55. Ibid., 154.

56. Ibid., 153.

57. Ibid., 12, 13.

58. Ibid., 14.

59. Ibid., 107–108.

60. Ibid., I:382.

61. Ibid., 383.

62. Ibid., 384.

63. Ibid., 384–405.

64. Ibid., 405–11.

65. Ibid., 406–407.

66. Ibid., 412.

67. Ibid., 413.

68. Ibid., 412–33.

69. Ibid., II:369.

70. Ibid., I: Editor's Appendix, 90–93.

71. Ibid.

72. Ibid., 94.

73. Ibid., 94, 96.

74. Ibid., I:x.

75. Ibid., III:201.

76. Ibid., III: Editor's Appendix, 11, 12; "An Act Directing the Course of Descents," 1785 *Virginia Acts* c. 60.

77. Tucker, *Blackstone's Commentaries,* III: Editor's Appendix, 12–52.

78. Ibid., 258.

79. Ibid., 3–10.

80. William Tatham to St. George Tucker, January 17, 1795, and January 30, 1795; Zephaniah Swift to St. George Tucker, June 1, 1796, Tucker-Coleman Collection, Earl Gregg Swem Library, College of William and Mary, Williamsburg, Virginia.

81. Abraham Small to St. George Tucker, April 7, 1802, ibid.,

82. St. George Tucker to Birch and Small, August 21, 1802, ibid.

83. Receipt and Note from Birch and Small to St. George Tucker, February 22, 1803., ibid.

84. Abraham Small to St. George Tucker, February 13, 1803, ibid.

85. "Names of the Subscribers," in William Blackstone, *Commentaries on the Laws of England,* 4 vols. (Philadelphia: Robert Bell, 1771–72); Waterman, 629, 630.

86. Cullen, *St. George Tucker,* 162.

87. Elizabeth Bauer, *Commentaries on the Constitution, 1790–1860,* Studies in History, Economics and Public Law, no. 575 (New York: Columbia University Press, 1952), 346.

88. Alfred Z. Reed, *Training for the Public Profession of the Law* (1921; reprint ed., New York: Arno Press, 1976), 117.

THOMAS P. SLAUGHTER

The Politics of Treason in the 1790s

ARTICLE III, Section 3, of the U.S. Constitution—the treason clause—was a mistake. It was the product of the founding fathers' ignorance of English statute law, and their wide—if in most cases shallow—acquaintance with the major common law commentaries, including those of Hale, Coke, Foster, and Blackstone. The commentators disagreed about some fundamental tenets of treason law, but collectively they gave American readers the impression that English prosecution of political crime was much less chaotic than even a cursory perusal of the state cases reveals.

The reality is that order, rationality, and linear progression over time were not the hallmarks of treason law during the centuries of English colonization of the New World or, for that matter, thereafter. The ambition of commentators to generalize about the common law—to find systematic evolution toward an ever-fairer, more orderly, more rational law that better protected the rights of Englishmen over time—was most ambitious and least successful for political crime. The founding fathers, however, did not realize these limitations or this flaw in the definition of the English law of treason as it was passed down to them by Blackstone and his predecessors.

The commentaries mark the point from which delegates to the constitutional convention *believed* that they were embarking on new law. In underestimating the chaos of English treason law, the commentators were thus actually helping to create law to the extent that their analyses became the basis for judicial and legislative understandings of treason's history and the dictates of precedent.

Federalists and Antifederalists alike were, of course, working in the realm of theory when they debated the potential impact of the Constitution on American law. The realities of the treason clause would be worked out on the battlefield and in the courts, in those moments of intense political turmoil that all the founding fathers most feared. James Wilson was a key transitional figure between the theoretical world of drafting the treason clause and the real world of enforcing it. Despite Wilson's defeat in the constitutional convention on amending the "two-witness" rule for treason convictions, he was most directly responsible for the remainder of the language and content of the treason clause. As a member of the committee of detail, Wilson apparently drafted the original version of Article III, Section 3, himself. Fortunately, we have the indirect but meaningful evidence of Wilson's law lectures delivered at the University of Pennsylvania between 1790 and 1792, from which we can discern his views on treason. Wilson's lectures are significant here not just for the light they shed on his role in drafting Article III, Section 3, but because as an associate justice of the Supreme Court shortly thereafter, he played a critical role in defining the Whiskey Rebellion riots of 1794 as the first mass treasonous offenses against the federal government under the Constitution. Thus, we do have some evidence bearing on the relationships between the drafters' intentions and subsequent applications of the law.

Reflecting his reliance on the British commentators rather than a close study of English case law, Wilson found much to admire in the evolution of the law of treason from the fourteenth century. As Wilson misunderstood the history of that process, the treason statute of Edward III had since served England "like a rock, strong by nature, and fortified, as successive occasions required, by the able and honest assistance of art." According to Wilson, who knew as much about British law as any American of his day, the English treason statute "has been impregnable by all the rude and boisterous assaults which have been made upon it at different quarters by ministers and by judges; and as an object of national security, as well as of national pride, it may well be styled the legal Gibraltar of England."[1]

In the eyes of its creator, the treason clause of the Constitution not only built on this solid English foundation, but strengthened it. Americans, like the British, were protected from the "judicial storms" associated with constructive treason. By eliminating the "monarchical parts" and securing protection from "legislative tempests," Wilson believed that the founding fathers had repaired the only structural defects in the English law. To Wilson, the terms of Article III, Section 3, were clear. He drew his definitions from the commentaries of Hale, Coke, Foster, and Blackstone, amending them as appropriate for a Republican nation lacking a monarch. Substituting "obedience" (to the nation) for "allegiance" (to the monarch), Wilson paraphrased Blackstone's answer to the rhetorical question, "By whom may war be levied?" "Of obedience the antipode is treason," Wilson argued. All who owe the United States obedience are capable of committing treason against it. All who receive its protection, Wilson reasoned, again relying on Blackstone, owe the nation obedience.[2]

Defining "levying war" seemed to Wilson a more complex problem, but again one that already had been resolved in English law as reported by the commentators. When people who owe the United States obedience are "arrayed in a warlike manner," to quote the normal form of an English indictment, war is legally levied. Borrowing directly from Hale, Wilson defined such an array:

> As where people are assembled in great numbers, armed with offensive weapons, or weapons of war, if they march thus armed in a body, if they have chosen commanders or officers, if they march with banners displayed, or with drums or trumpets: whether the greatness of their numbers and their continuance together doing these acts may not amount to being arrayed in a warlike manner, deserves consideration. If they have no military arms, nor march or continue together in the posture of war; they may be great rioters, but their conduct does not always amount to a levying of war.[3]

The *illusion* of precision here did not entirely escape Wilson, any more than it had escaped Foster, upon whom he relied for a clarification of the fuzzy line between riot and insurrection, between disturbing the peace and treason. According to Foster and Wilson, levying war to redress a private wrong, in response to a private quarrel, or to take revenge against particular persons could not be construed as treason under either English or American law. A warlike array that addressed a private claim or that aimed to rescue particular persons from incarceration did not seem treasonous to these legal scholars. On the other hand, "insurrections in order to throw down all inclosures, to open all prisons, to enhance the price of all labor, to expel foreigners in general, or those from any single nation living under the protection of government, to alter the established law, or to render it ineffectual—insurrections to accomplish these ends, by numbers and an open and armed force, are a levying of war against the United States."[4]

In the end, though, and unlike most modern legal historians, Wilson had to admit that "the line of division between this species of treason and an aggravated riot is sometimes very fine and difficult to be distinguished." He apparently recognized that one person's "warlike array" could be another's spontaneous gathering. What about a case where the "particular individual" who is a victim of mob violence is an officer of the government? Clearly, an armed array designed to "alter the established law" could be defined as treason, but what about such cases as those debated by the legal historians Bradley Chapin and James Willard Hurst, where one particular law is under attack, but obedience to the remaining body of established law is not challenged? Is assemblage in "warlike array" necessary or sufficient evidence of treason? Or might mere words—spoken, written, or published—suffice as evidence not just of intent, but as an "overt act" under the Constitution's definition? Wilson does not say, and thus the intentions of the drafters in these matters, if any of these questions even occurred to them, are not accessible to us. They all are, however, questions that came before federal courts during the federalist era. And where the answers seemed unclear, the courts did not always take Wilson's advice that "in such instances, it is safest and most prudent to consider the case in question as lying on the side of the inferior crime."[5]

The treason trials resulting from the Whiskey Rebellion represented the first test of the "levying law" component of the treason clause and thus give the earliest clues to the operative meanings of Article III, Section 3. At issue in the trials was (1) the strictness with which procedural protections for the accused would be respected by the courts; (2) the meaning of "overt act"; (3) definition of the line between riot and rebellion; and (4) the authority of the courts to engage in constructing treasons.

Most instructive in these regards are the trials of Philip Vigol and John Mitchell, the two "rebels" convicted of treason and eventually pardoned by President Washington. In each case, the prosecution had fallen short of the procedures outlined by Congress for trying capital crimes, but the judges were not about to dismiss such politically significant charges on merely procedural grounds. And, in light of the highly charged political atmosphere in which the court deliberated, it is not surprising that the judges displayed throughout the proceedings a stronger sympathy for the prosecution than the defense. The government felt vulnerable to both domestic violence and international intrigue. The judiciary was being asked to play an important, perhaps a decisive, role in demonstrating the new nation's strength before a large audience of dissident Americans and a hostile diplomatic corps.

In the era of the French Revolution, the Washington administration had reasonable grounds to fear for the very lives of government officials and to wonder whether the administrative and judicial branches established by the Constitution could cooperate in moments of severe stress. But the army had failed to capture any of the "leaders" of the "rebellion." It had left Judges Peters and Paterson with about twenty obscure characters in custody to shoulder the blame for seven thousand "rebels" and to justify the tremendous expense of marching an army of 12,950 men, an array larger than the average daily troop strength of the continental forces in the American revolution, to suppress this "treasonous" assault on federal tax collectors in western Pennsylvania.

Observers of the trials from among Philadelphia's legal profession theorized that Judge Peters authorized the detention of so many unlikely villains because of political rather than strictly legal motives. They knew in advance, as Peters must have, that the overwhelming proportion could not be convicted no matter how sympathetically the judges responded to the prosecution, and in fact few were ever brought to trial. But the times demanded scapegoats. The army, the administration, and the eastern citizenry required symbols of their victory over enemies of the state.

Lawyers witnessing the trials of Vigol and Mitchell reported that the verdicts were inescapable, given the judges' behavior. Clearly, the judges had decided that these were going to be the government's best cases and if they were to achieve at least token convictions, it would have to be here. Paterson, who was an associate justice of the supreme court, instructed Vigol's jury that "with respect to the evidence, the current runs one way; it harmonizes in all its parts." Likewise, the jury was told, "with respect to [Vigol's] intention . . . there is not, unhappily, the slightest possibility of doubt. . . . The crime is proved." Dutifully, the jury agreed; and the judiciary was spared the embarrassment of total failure.

The government had its examples, and the president an occasion for a magnanimous gesture, when he pardoned the two convicted traitors. Just as Alexander Hamilton had anticipated in his defense of the pardoning power in *Federalist* 73, a moment had arisen when political exigencies seemed best served by a combination of decisive action—arrest, trial, conviction, and sentencing—accompanied by the merciful hand of the president.[6]

The treason trials were more, though, than acts in a political theater. Enduring, or at least evolving, law was being made in regard to key elements of the Constitution's treason clause. Defining "levying war" was of particular concern and the arguments of respective counsel demonstrate that there was no universal or settled understanding of the term. The outcome of the cases reveals that the definition accepted by the court was much broader and less protective of individuals than is generally assumed.

The prosecutor, John Rawle, in *U.S. v. Mitchell* contended that the term had the same meaning in the Constitution as in English law, a point that the defense did not contest. He trotted out Hale, Foster, and Blackstone, among other commentators, and referred to particular English state trials in framing the broadest conceivable definition. "By the English authorities," Rawle contended, "it is uniformly and clearly declared, that raising a body of men to obtain by intimidation or violence the repeal of a law, or to oppose and prevent by force or terror the execution of the law, is an act of levying war." An assembly "armed and arrayed in a warlike manner" was enough to constitute treason, according to Foster. Although conspiracy was not alone enough, Rawle allowed, if any of the conspirators committed an overt act of levying war, all the conspirators, regardless of their actual presence, or even their support of the act, were equally complicit. Likewise, joining the array after the plot had been hatched was nonetheless treasonous, "for in treason all are principals."[7]

Mitchell's attorney acknowledged that an attempt to compel Congress to repeal a statute by violence or intimidation is an act of treason. Defense counsel either did not notice or did not care to engage frontally Rawle's significant embellishment of Blackstone's definition in his substitution of resistance to "a law" for the English commentator's more general requisite resistance to "law." The significance here, of course, is that it was not at all clear from the English commentators, including Foster and Blackstone, whether resistance to a single law, in a manner that did not pose a violent threat to the enacting body, constituted treason.

On the general question, though, the defense did contest whether "resisting execution of a law, or attempting to coerce an officer into the resignation of a commission" amounted to treason. Here the defense was attempting to make the same broad distinction that Hale, Foster, and Blackstone made between general opposition to law (which was treason) and a specific act against a specific law (which was not). "Let it be granted," the defense argued, ". . . that an insurrection for an avowed purpose of suppressing all the excise offices in the United States, may be construed into an act of levying war against the government . . . it does not follow that an attempt to oblige one officer to resign, or to suppress all the offices in one [tax collecting] district, will be a crime of the same denomination."[8]

Likewise, the defense and prosecution offered very different interpretations of "overt act." It seemed to the defense that the prosecution's more open-ended definition left room for constructive, or interpretive, treasons, which are "the dread and scourge of any nation that allows them." It could be proved by testimony of the requisite two witnesses that Mitchell attended a public meeting prior to the attack and burning of the tax supervisor's house. Only one witness placed Mitchell at the house burning, "alone, at a distance of about thirty or forty rods; and it is not recollected whether he had a gun." Another witness vaguely recollected seeing him on the road to the house with the mob.

The prosecution sought to define the overt act constructively to include both events—the meeting at which Mitchell, among many others, was heard to express opinions of a "treasonous" design and the burning of excise inspector Neville's house—as part of one overt act that also included a subsequent gathering at a later date. Despite some heavy drinking and violent posturing by a legion of hostile rural folks, it broke up without incident.[9]

Justice Paterson, in his charge to Mitchell's jury, accepted the prosecution's argument in toto. He instructed jurors that the object of the riots was clearly "of a general and public nature," and was, therefore, treason. Paterson drew on Foster's distinction between public and private grievances to redefine virtually all acts of public violence aimed at specific laws, regulations, or officials as treasonous. And he seemed to leave room within his definition of treason even for riots aimed at nongovernmental agencies or individuals. Indeed, Paterson's notion of "levying war" harkened back to the seventeenth century and was as expansive as any pronounced from an Anglo-American bench since the Glorious Revolution. All rioters who focused their violence either against the government or attempted by extralegal means to obstruct a normal governmental function—what Paterson termed "usurpation of the authority of government"—could by his definition be prosecuted under the treason clause. This jury charge thus reflected not only the flexibility of Article III, Section 3, for meeting threats perceived by federal officials, but the distance between elite sanction of some urban crowd activity in the prerevolutionary years, and the fear and intolerance of all mobs by Federalist politicians during the era of the French Revolution.[10]

Having defined "levying war" in a manner that, in Paterson's mind, inescapably described a series of events in western Pennsylvania during the summer of 1794, he next proceeded to explain "overt act" to the jurors in a way that just as surely included Mitchell's role in the rebellion. It seemed to the judge that whichever definition of a general or specific overt act the jury accepted, Mitchell was guilty of treason. If the defendant was present at the Braddock's field assembly, as four witnesses concurred that he was, that was enough in the judge's mind to convict for treason. It was of no relevance that the armed array gathered there committed no act of violence toward the government, *if* Mitchell's *intention* in attending the assembly was treasonous. Reasoning backward from this event to the meeting at Couche's Fort, at which multiple witnesses placed Mitchell, the judge found abundant evidence of treasonous intent and saw no reason not to draw connections between the Couche's Fort meeting, the burning of Neville's house, and the Braddock's field assembly as a divisible, but single, overt act.[11]

It was of no account to Justice Paterson that the prosecution had failed to produce two witnesses to Mitchell's presence at Neville's house on the day of the only overtly violent act in the scenario, since the "overt act" encompassed all three events, transcended the time and place of any one of them, and could be fulfilled by presence at one alone. So much for the traditional legal historians' assertion that constructive treason was eliminated from American law by the Constitution! So much for the anachronistic vision of the "narrow" definition of "levying war," the two witness rule, and "overt act" portions of the treason clause. When "overt act" can be defined as broadly as Justice Paterson construed it in *U.S. v. Mitchell*, the Constitution's two witness rule represents no obvious advance over the English statute of William III. If an overt act can be judicially constructed over time and place, the Constitution's language dictating that there must be two witnesses to the same overt act carries little more restrictive weight against the government's case than the English law's requirement that there must be at least two witnesses to the same general act of treason.

The trials of Vigol and Mitchell were not anomalies in the history of American law. The decisions of Judge Peters and Justice Paterson set precedents that guided subsequent jurists in their efforts to interpret the treason clause. Their definitions of "overt act" and "levying war" were particularly influential. Four years later, in 1799, Judge Peters, this time sitting with associate justice of the Supreme Court James Iredell, was called upon in *U.S. v. John Fries* to preside over a major treason case that had striking parallels to the Whiskey Rebellion trials in its issues, judicial rulings, results, and the external political pressures under which the case was tried.

The occasion for Fries's alleged treason was again opposition to a federal tax, this time an internal tax on houses rather than whiskey. The center of opposition was again Pennsylvania, but this time in three eastern rather than four western counties of the state. "Fries' Rebellion," as the government labeled it, was also known locally and in the opposition press as the "Hot Water War." This title was intended to ridicule the Adams administration's gross overreaction to what some people saw as, at worst, a humorous if overzealous expression of free speech. Granted, at least one woman had thrown a bucket of hot water from an upstairs window of her house onto a taxman who was trying to assess property values by counting panes. Other housewives (most of them German) had also "treated the invaders of their fire-sides with every species of indignity, resisting . . . the measurement of their windows by all the domestic artillery." Equally uncontested was the fact that tax collectors in Bucks, Montgomery, and Northampton Counties had been harassed, ridiculed, and threatened by men who described themselves as "sons of liberty" and "whiskey boys."

Finally, and most seriously, a crowd of about one hundred persons, of which Fries was the putative leader, did "rescue" about eighteen men from a federal marshal and his deputies. The prisoners were being housed at a tavern overnight en route to Philadelphia for trial on charges stemming from their opposition to the house tax.[12]

No shots were fired; no one was injured; and the prisoners, who apparently did not wish to be rescued, later made their way unescorted to Philadelphia where they surrendered to the law. Nonetheless, President Adams felt compelled to request five hundred militiamen to put down the "rebellion," at a cost of about $80,000 to the federal government. The troops met no resistance upon their arrival and had little to do save terrorizing the local people, knocking down liberty poles, posting the president's proclamation in German and English, and sweeping up "traitors" to be tried in federal courts. There was some suggestion by those unfriendly to the Adams administration that the subsequent treason trials represented an attempt to suppress political opposition in this Republican stronghold and to justify the cost of persecuting some of the president's political enemies.[13]

In any event, Fries was charged and twice convicted of treason by levying war against the United States.[14] His defense counsel in the first trial argued that what the federal government was attempting was no less than a "novel experiment" in the history of Anglo-American law. Ignoring the clear precedent of English treason law that "the resistance of no law is treason, but the militia law," the prosecution sought to define riot and rescue, crimes covered perfectly well as misdemeanors under the sedition act recently adopted by Congress, as a combined capital offense. Relying on precedents from the trials of Vigol and Mitchell, the prosecution seemed bent on vitiating the Constitution's limiting clauses relating to the overt act, and to give the courts almost unlimited potential to construct treasons from a series of less serious crimes. The defense never denied that Fries was guilty of several lesser offenses, indeed they acknowledged it. The lawyers simply asserted that their client should not be executed for treason, as that crime was described in the Constitution and understood under established Anglo-American definitions.[15]

For the most part, the defense lawyers were better historians than the prosecution, which is another way of saying that from a modern perspective the weight of history balanced in Fries's favor.[16] Nor did the defense misrepresent the government's case. Prosecution attorneys did not respond to defense contentions with a list of parallel cases from English law. Indeed, they readily acknowledged that an overt act by rescue of prisoners was a new, and thus perhaps a more sinister, method of acting out treasonous designs.[17]

In other respects, the prosecution arguments were a reprise of those presented in the Whiskey Rebellion cases, as one might expect, given their success in the Mitchell and Vigol trials, the obvious parallels of tax resistance cases, and the presence of Judge Peters, whose views were known and who had ruled favorably on the same prosecution arguments in the earlier trials. Indeed, the prosecution's definition of treason by levying war was a paraphrase of the judges' instructions to juries in the previous cases. According to this reading of the treason clause, group violence aimed at any law or laws of the United States or designed for any public end that usurped the rightful prerogatives of government falls under the larger definition. It is the intention behind the action, rather than the overt act in isolation, that defines the crime.

Under some circumstances, riot or rescue might be deemed misdemeanors, but when the design is "to defeat the operation of the laws," then the crime is treason. In the specific case of Fries, he was known to have participated in meetings that culminated in a written document (that the prosecution could not produce) expressing animosity to the tax law. At those same meetings, Fries's statements against the tax law were "extremely violent, and he threatened to shoot one of the assessors, Mr. Foulke, through the legs, if he did proceed to assess the houses." Fries was also known to have threatened another assessor that "he should be committed to an old stable, and there fed on rotten corn." On yet another occasion, Fries was heard to say that he would not submit to the law and that he could raise seven hundred men in opposition by the next morning. In a fit of anger, the defendant had also made statements to the effect that "it should soon be in this country as it was in France." Fries warned tax men that they might be injured if they continued in their line of work. Witnesses attested that Fries, armed with "a large pistol," had assembled fifty to sixty men, "the greatest part of whom were in arms," to prevent the assessors from going about their business in Bucks County.[18]

The parallels to the Whiskey Rebellion cases were so close, as the prosecution portrayed them, to preclude any doubt of the appropriate verdict here. Resistance to a law; intimidation or assault on government officials; and assembly in martial array with the intention of subverting the law, even in the absence of overt violence, had already been determined twice in federal courts to sustain a treason charge under the Constitution. The government's case against Fries, as the prosecution (as well as the defense) well knew, was in important respects significantly stronger than those that had convicted Vigol and Mitchell. There was no problem finding two witnesses to a clearly defined overt act—the rescue of prisoners at Bethlehem on March 7—as there had been in the Mitchell case. Furthermore, the rescue was an even "more violent breach of the law than the attack on Nevil[le]'s house" (to which Mitchell had been linked by only one witness) in the sense that Fries and the mob had defied and abused not just a government official, but an officer of the law.[19]

Judge Peters, in his instructions to the jury, summarized the case decisively in the prosecution's favor. It is treason by levying war, he told the jurors, "for persons *who have not but a common interest with their fellow-citizens,* to oppose or prevent, by force, numbers or intimidation, a *public* and *general* law of the United States, *with intent* to prevent its operation, or compel its repeal. Force is necessary to complete the crime; but the quantum of force is immaterial." In restating his views, and those of Justice Paterson, from the Mitchell case, Peters was paraphrasing the English commentators' distinction between violence to right a private wrong and that which has a public purpose. Peters was taking Blackstone's reference to treasonous "general" opposition to law, which might fairly be restated as "general opposition to law," and recasting it into his own unique configuration of violent opposition to any "general law" as treason.[20]

This was a creative and astoundingly expansive interpretation of the English jurist's meaning. But the logic was a coherent outgrowth of the commentator's argument: "if numbers and force can render one law ineffectual, which is tantamount to its repeal, the whole system of laws may be destroyed in detail." The infamous seventeenth-century English Judge Jeffreys could not have put it better himself! There is no lesser crime where opposition to the government is concerned; the only distinctions are acts of magnanimity by the state. The practice of Parliament responding to the "public opinion" of the London mob was an act of grace (or an acknowledgment of impotence), not a recognition of right, and a dangerous precedent that had no place under the more representative form of government enjoyed in the United States. Justice Iredell implicitly sustained this reading by describing his ideas on points of treason law as "absolutely" coinciding with those of Peters, to whom he deferred on such matters.[21]

Finally, there was the ugly issue of "constructive" treason that the defense had raised in the course of its argument that the government seemed bent on returning American law to the dark days of the Stuart kings. Peters admitted that "the doctrine of *constructive treason* has produced much real mischief in another country." He acknowledged that he and his fellow judges in the Whiskey Rebellion and Fries's rebellion cases were engaged in constructive interpretations of the crime of treason. And yet it seemed to Peters "not fair and sound reasoning to argue against the necessary and indispensable *use* of construction, from the *abuses* it has produced." The appropriate lesson to be taken from former abuses is that jurists must be cautious in their constructions, "but not so much alarmed about *abuses* as to restrain from the proper and necessary *use* of interpretation."

In more modern parlance, Peters and Iredell were not "strict constructionists" of the Constitution. They found ample room for reasoned and reasonable amplification of the language of the treason clause. They felt bound by neither the weight of English precedent nor the intentions of those who had drafted the clause.[22]

After the conviction, at the point of sentencing, defense counsel presented evidence that a juror expressed severe prejudice against Fries before the trial, and after he had been selected for the case. Judge Peters thought that insufficient cause for retrial, but relented in response to Justice Iredell's wishes. In the second trial, not surprisingly, the prosecution rested its case on the same judicial principles and logic that had prevailed the first time around. The significance of this second trial for a historical consideration of treason law rests less, then, on the judicial rationales used to reach the same verdict, than on the behavior of the presiding judge.[23]

Fries ended up without an attorney in his second trial. Associate justice of the supreme court Samuel Chase thus served multiple roles as judge (along with district judge Peters) and counsel to the defendant. Defense lawyers resigned in protest when Chase presented a written opinion on the law of treason at the beginning of the trial, thereby vitiating any possibility of a defense based on the law rather than the facts of the case. Lawyers for the defense refused to resume their places when Chase offered to withdraw his statement, and they privately advised Fries not to accept court-appointed counsel. Fries's counsel apparently reasoned that the facts of the case were not in dispute. Since the judge had ruled on the law prior to their arguments, their client had no defense whatever. It was in Fries's best interests, as his lawyers calculated it, to contribute to creating a situation in which there was the appearance of an unfair trial, thus establishing grounds for appeal or, better yet, a popular uproar that would lead to a pardon of Fries after the inevitable conviction and death sentence.

The plan worked, as President Adams's change of heart on the necessity for token executions suggests. The unpopularity of the president's decision to pardon Fries (and the two others convicted of treason) within his cabinet and the Federalist party testifies to the political atmosphere in which the trials were conducted. The clamor for pardon in Pennsylvania and from Republican politicians and newspaper editors illustrates the contending pressures under which Adams (and the judges) labored. And the president's consultation with the defense attorneys prior to his decision highlights his attempt to balance legal, humanitarian, and political concerns in this sensitive case. In retrospect, it appears that Adams was in a no-win situation. His pardon of Fries made few, if any, converts from among his detractors within the Republican camp and alienated further those Federalists who increasingly doubted his capacity to lead.

The case also had repercussions for Justice Chase, who was tried by the U.S. Senate for high crimes and misdemeanors in 1804. The first of eight articles of impeachment addressed his behavior on the bench during Fries's second trial. A Republican Congress charged the Federalist judge with being in the Fries's case, "highly arbitrary, oppressive and unjust." Specifically, the Senate committee accused him of prejudicing the jury against Fries by delivering a written opinion on the law before defense arguments on those points; refusing defense counsel the freedom to cite English precedents where they found them relevant to the case; and barring the defense from addressing questions of law. In sum, his accusers charged Chase with having disgraced "the character of the American bench, in manifest violation of law and justice, and in open contempt of the rights of juries, on which ultimately rest the liberty and safety of the American people."[24]

There was, of course, no questioning of Chase's interpretation of Article III, Section 3, his defense of judicially constructed treason, or his understanding of the relationship between English and American treason law. The law of treason apparently did not define one of the ideological fissures between Federalists and Republicans. More clearly, it highlighted conflict between the two parties: "outs" (Antifederalists, proto-Republicans, and others who fell outside the real and philosophical contours of power during the Washington and Adams administrations). They were attempting to define legitimate and successful methods for overturning the political status quo. And "ins," who sought, in an age that was only beginning to credit the existence of political parties, to use the courts as one means to establish and extend their rule across time and space.

The politics of this struggle became even more clearly expressed in treason law as control of the executive—and then legislative—branch was wrested from Federalists by the Republicans beginning in 1801. For the first time in its history the nation was faced with a judiciary, which remained overwhelmingly Federalist, out of sympathy with the president *and* Congress. The impeachment and trial of Chase was one significant illustration of interbranch conflict. The primacy of Fries's treason trial in the charges against Chase reflects the symbolic and real significance of Federalist use (and, in the eyes of Republicans, abuse) of the treason charge for political ends, as well as the Republicans' eagerness to use the courts against their opponents. And the inability to convict Chase in the Senate on close votes testifies to the transitional and incomplete status of the transfer of power.[25]

Ironically, and at least partly as a function of this ongoing conflict among the branches of government, it would be a Federalist judge who began the process of narrowing the scope of treason law. He, for the first time, sought to define clear limits to the authority of the state and broader rights and protections for those rights as they were contested in treason trials. Only when judges began, like John Marshall, to conceive of executive and legislative behavior as oppressive in theory and practice, would they start to take more literally the "narrow" definition of treason that subsequent judges and legal historians have found embodied in Article III, Section 3, of the Constitution.

It would be federal judges following Marshall's lead, who charted a more independent course for the federal judiciary. It would be judges working in an ever-more pluralistic political society, who whittled away at the definitions of "levying war" and "overt act," who discovered the obvious and literal meanings of *two* witnesses to *one* act that established the modern law of treason. Our more recent understandings of Article III, Section 3, are not—as both traditionalists and revisionists among legal historians would have it—legacies of the Federalist era. The modern law of treason is, rather, a consequence of a historical process in which the Federalist era played a significant role—a process of conflict and change responding to political contingencies and social pressures that give our law meaning as a part, rather than apart from, ongoing struggles for power and precedence in the United States.

NOTES

1. James DeWitt Andrews, ed., *The Works of James Wilson* (Chicago, 1896), II, 413.
2. Ibid., 414, 415, 416, 417.
3. Ibid., 418.
4. Ibid., 419–20.
5. Ibid., 420. Wilson apparently recognized that the treason clause did a better job of protecting American citizens from what he termed "legislative tempests" than from judicial constructions of treason, but he also believed that Americans were far better protected from odious judicial constructions of treason than the British were during the seventeenth century. See "Charge of the Hon. James Wilson, esq. Judge of the Federal Court for the District

of Pennsylvania, to the Grand Jury of said court, Delivered April 12, 1790," [Carey's] *American Museum* 7 (1790): Appendix II, Public Papers, 40.

6. Alexander James Dallas, reporter, *Reports of Cases Ruled and Adjudged in the Courts of Pennsylvania, Before and Since the Revolution* (Philadelphia, 1790), II, 346, 347.

7. Ibid., 349.

8. Ibid., 351.

9. Ibid., 350, 352.

10. Ibid., 355.

11. Ibid., 356.

12. Francis Wharton, *State Trials of the United States During the Administrations of Washington and Adams* (1849; rpt. ed., New York, 1970), 458n. The number of prisoners rescued at Bethlehem has been variously estimated in the secondary sources as three, eighteen, twenty, and twenty-three. The source of the confusion is unclear. There was undoubtedly an ethnic component to the protests, with Germans, many of whom apparently misunderstood the nature of the tax, taking the lead. Fries himself, however, was of Welsh ancestry.

13. William W. H. Davis, *The Fries Rebellion, 1798–99* (1899; rpt. ed., New York, 1969); Peter Levine, "The Fries Rebellion: Social Violence and the Politics of the New Nation," *Pennsylvania History* 40 (1973): 241–58; Jane Shaffer Elsmere, "The Trials of John Fries," *Pennsylvania Magazine of History and Biography* 103 (1979): 432–45; Dwight F. Henderson, "Treason, Sedition, and Fries' Rebellion," *American Journal of Legal History* 14 (1970): 308–17. In fact, and to the great embarrassment and disbelief of the government, Fries and several other "leaders" of the unrest were Federalists. One contemporary noted that on this issue the two political factions were united in Bucks and Northampton Counties: "the Tories were opposed to the tax and the Whigs to the assessors." Cited in Davis, *Fries Rebellion,* 103. It appears that the Alien and Sedition Acts and the window tax were decisive in converting these prosperous eastern Pennsylvania Germans to the Jeffersonian-Republican cause. See Manning J. Dauer, *The Adams Federalists* (Baltimore, 1953), 280.

14. The second trial was necessitated by a successful defense motion for a new trial. Only after the first trial ended, argued defense lawyers, had they been able to secure testimony that one of the jurors had openly and repeatedly declared a prejudice against the accused after he was on the jury. After considering the arguments of defense and prosecution attorneys, Judge Peters found insufficient cause for a new trial, but Justice Iredell was persuaded and Peters relented. See Thomas Carpenter, stenographer, *The Two Trials of John Fries on an Indictment of Treason; Together With a Brief Report of the Trials of Several Other Persons, for Treason and Insurrection* (Philadelphia, 1800), Appendix II, 11–45. According to Henderson, "Treason, Sedition, and Fries' Rebellion," 312, there were eleven treason indictments, forty-four for conspiracy; thirty-two for conspiracy, rescue, and obstruction of process; and one for seditious expressions. At the time and since, jurists have drawn on both Fries's first and second trials for their understandings of the law of treason in the early republic. The first trial is actually a better guide to the range of arguments and decisions that would influence subsequent interpretations of Article III, Section 3. The arguments were developed more fully in the first trial, there were no defense lawyers in the second trial, and Judge Chase's behavior in the second trial was seen to be an anomaly, the most clever example of the potential for judicial abuse of treason law on American record.

15. Carpenter, *Two Trials,* 148. The government did use the sedition act to prosecute other participants in Fries's rebellion, but sought to make special examples of Fries and

several other "leaders" of the unrest. See Henderson, "Treason, Sedition, and Fries' Rebellion," 312, 314. In addition to Fries, Frederick Hearny and John Gettman were also convicted of treason. All three men were pardoned by President Adams. Stenographic notes of the other treason trials apparently were not taken.

16. That is to say, the weight of history balanced in Fries's favor if one accepts the premise of lawyers on both sides that the law of treason had over its history a higher rationality than merely providing a public theater for labeling as illegitimate all threats to rulers and dispatching those so defined in what was perceived by the rulers to be the most politically efficacious manner.

17. Carpenter, *Two Trials,* 160.

18. Ibid., 19, 20–24.

19. Ibid., 163.

20. Ibid., 204.

21. Ibid., 205, 164–65. Justice Iredell's interpretation of the treason clause in this case appears much more expansive than his general remarks to a South Carolina grand jury suggested several years before the trial of Fries. See [Carey's] *American Museum,* 12 (1795): 36.

22. Ibid., 206–207.

23. Ibid., Appendix II, 11–45.

24. Charles Evans, stenographer, *Report of the Trial of the Hon. Samuel Chase* (Baltimore, 1805), Appendix, 3–4.

25. The House of Representative favored impeachment of Chase by a 73 to 32 vote. The Senate, in which Republicans also outnumbered Federalists by a considerable margin, failed narrowly to secure the two-thirds vote necessary for conviction. The process by which Chase narrowly escaped conviction on the impeachment charges testifies to the transitional and incomplete process of the transfer of power and to how much the Republican leadership had yet to learn about managing floor votes in the upper house. See Melvin I. Urovsky, *A March of Liberty: A Constitutional History of the United States* (New York: 1988), 189–91. Richard Ellis, "The Impeachment of Samuel Chase," in Michal R. Belknap, ed., *American Political Trials* (Westport, Conn., 1981), 57–78.

ELISABETH A. CAWTHON

Rough Work and Tough Logic: The English Roots of Texas Workers' Compensation Law

IT IS NOT as far as one might think from the royal courts in London to the halls of justice in Texas. Workers' compensation is an area in which American courts and English courts often have looked to each other for precedents. American state legislatures frequently have studied English legislation, in drafting their own bills. England and America have paralleled and echoed one another in the legal treatment of "the wounded soldiers of industry," throughout the nineteenth and twentieth centuries.

What accounts for that doctrinal interdependence between nations, which by the 1830s were long since politically independent? The general principle of a common legal heritage binding England and the former English North American colonies at times was invoked by lawmakers on both sides of the Atlantic as they discussed worker's compensation. Foremost on their minds, however, were more practical matters. As Anglo-American lawmakers considered worker's compensation law, their discussions revolved around the apportionment of the costs of industrial development.

Those are current concerns as well. Workers' compensation law in states across the union, including Texas, still is a topic of much comment among not only legal scholars but employees, employers, politicians, insurers, and medical people. In describing the law of workers' compensation, one commentator observed that "there were few to praise and none to love it."[1] Many Texans would continue to agree. Employees often criticize the Texas workers' compensation system as not providing remedy enough when they suffer terrible physical injuries due to their employers' negligence. Employers consider it either intrusive in the employer-employee relationship or cumbersome because of the paperwork it entails. Lawyers see it as circumventing the process of civil recovery for injuries, and as not providing enough opportunity for jury trials. Medical personnel view it as divisive because it reinforces divisions between company doctors and independent physicians. Insurers maintain that the Texas system makes the cost of their doing business in Texas greater. Other reservations—for instance, among civic leaders—include the contention that the cost of workers' compensation is so high in Texas that businesses locate outside the state, because of it.[2]

The law of workers' compensation is not only controversial. It is difficult for even specialists to summarize, because it is expressed legislatively, administratively, and judicially. State systems of compensation have been set up through legislation such as the Texas Workmen's Compensation Acts of 1913 and 1917. (State legislation must comport with applicable federal law, such as the Federal Employers' Liability Act of 1908.) Most recent state statutes not only set forth rules for employee recovery, but mandate an administrative system—including worker's compensation boards—which processes workplace accident claims.

The accumulated decisions of administrative agencies, such as the Texas Workers' Compensation Board, therefore, are a second type of law relevant to the compensation process. The decisions of judges in negligence suits provide a third venue in which workers' compensation law is made. When courts hear claims for damages against employers in cases brought by injured employees, or by their relatives in the event of occupational deaths, they add to the judge-made law of workers' compensation.[3]

Compensation schemes as established in state legislation allow employers to join a system authorized by the legislature and run by state administrative agencies. If employers do not tell the state of Texas otherwise, workers will be enrolled in the Texas workers' compensation system. If they choose to opt out of state compensation, then the state of Texas assumes that when people who work for that employer are injured on the job, the employer will face civil suits for damages from employees.

The state of Texas encourages employers to participate in its system, through legislative provisions that employers who "opt out" will not be able to defend themselves against employee suits, with certain arguments, which are part of the common law of England and a number of American states. (States such as Texas are even stricter toward employers when employees are killed on the job. In certain instances of employee deaths, even employers who have signed up to belong to the state worker's compensation system can be sued.)

If, however, as most employers do, an employer decides to be part of the workers' compensation system in Texas, then several things will certainly occur, in the event that one of his employees is hurt—rather than killed—at work. A "covered" employer will not be open to a civil suit by his or her employee. The employee will be paid compensation because of injuries out of a fund administered by the state of Texas.

That sum of money is carefully specified by the state in a complicated set of tables, which taken into account lost wages, medical expenses, and even the value of certain parts of the body. Such specifications make for grisly reading; a finger is valued at a certain amount, and a hand a bit more, and a leg at yet another rate. This listing of missing limbs has ancient echoes; it is reminiscent of the Anglo-Saxon dooms, which specified *wergelds*, or "man-money," for personal injuries. One might expect that workers' compensation would have certain gruesome aspects, but how did the current Texas system become so unsatisfying to practically everyone associated with it?

Workers' compensation law in Texas has evolved through several distinct stages: one before Texas joined the union, one from about 1846 to about 1913, and one from the early 1900s through today. In legal treatises and even in indices to law reports, the terms that have been used to describe and categorize the law now termed "workers' compensation" have changed. Law students in the 1820s would have studied "the law of master and servant." By the late 1800s, the preferred description among legal scholars would have been "the law of employer liability." In the twentieth century, the phrase "workman's compensation law" is the usual one, although quite recently it is expressed as "workers' compensation."[4]

Those four different terms have been used by lawyers in Texas and elsewhere to refer to the legal ramifications when an employee is injured at work and decides to hold his or her employer accountable. For historians those terms are signposts. Understanding the shift from "masters and servants" to "employer liability," and from "employer liability" to "workmen's compensation," provides insight into several important historical questions. Those changes in legal terminology were the result of transformations in relationships between employers and employees, alterations in the scope of authority of legal institutions (such as the judiciary, juries, and legislatures), and a growing recognition of the power of the state to oversee the health and welfare of its citizens.

Prior to annexation in 1845, Texas legal forms were heavily influenced by Spain and Mexico. Spanish colonial justice was in many ways different from the legal institutions of the Anglo-American colonies. The legal rules covering workplace accidents prior to 1835 in Texas would have come under the branch of Spanish law regulating contracts—specifically contracts of employment.[5] Texas had claimed independence ten years before it became a state. Even earlier the area had shed some of the vestiges of Spanish law, especially during the increased migration of Anglo-Americans into Texas between 1825 and 1836. When Texas became a part of the union, Texans officially began to draw upon English common law for fundamental principles in judicial cases.[6] The very year that Texas joined the union, 1845, was a pivotal time in regard to legal doctrine, in England and therefore in the United States and in Texas.

Prior to the 1830s and 40s, the branch of Anglo-American law that would have applied to workplace accidents was known as the "law of master and servant." One very important idea that was continually cited, whenever cases of this sort were decided prior to the 1830s in either England or its former North American colonies, was a principle referred to as *respondeat superior.* Respondeat superior meant "let the master answer." It signified that employers had a duty to assist those who worked for them, in the event that employees were injured.[7]

The phrases that judges and other legal commentators used when writing about employer-employee relationships were very telling. Legal sources from the era prior to the 1830s describe not so much employers and employees as masters and servants. Several judges, in making decisions involving the doctrine of respondeat superior, spoke of employers' duties as familial in nature. Legal authorities were describing a fatherly duty by employers, to look after the members of their households, including their workers.[8] This paternalistic ideology befitted the highly personal nature of economic relationships in the preindustrial period, though it was to become outmoded during the Victorian age.[9] Far and away the largest single group of employees in England were domestic servants—household workers. In Texas before the 1830s most white workers also were employed in settings that were small-scale—as farm laborers, domestic servants, on board ships, or in small enterprises.[10]

How would respondeat superior have played out, in a hypothetical case from the 1820s in England, involving an employee's falling from scaffolding that his employer had bought and designed? The injured employee could have used the doctrine of respondeat superior to argue that his employer owed him a duty to have provided him with safe tools and a safe work place in which to labor. The case probably would have turned on the fact that his employer had not done those things, and the employer could have been held liable.

Most workers, however, did not go so far as to sue their employers when something tragic occurred at work. There were very practical reasons for failure to sue. A civil suit took money, first of all. The costs of a suit could amount to considerably more than a working person's annual income.[11] It was daunting to sue one's employer, given laborers' dependence on their employers. Often, the best witnesses in employer negligence cases were people who still worked for the person alleged to have been at fault. Were fellow workers going to risk their jobs in order to help their injured colleagues? In dangerous industries such as construction, the immediate self-interest of not endangering one's own job usually prevailed.

The idea of respondeat superior did not always allow employees to recover damages, even when they did muster the courage to sue their employers and gain the support of their fellow workers. There were several exceptions to respondeat superior, in the judge-made law. The doctrine of respondeat superior, for example, did not cover employees who were in certain occupations, such as sailors.[12] In the early nineteenth century, suits for occupational injuries were rare, compared with the actual occurrence of accidents. The rhetoric of respondeat superior was striking, however, for courts were saying that employers had a responsibility to help their workers.

In the 1830s in England and slightly later in the United States, the principle of respondeat superior was replaced. At first, it seemed as though judges were merely making certain exceptions to respondeat superior—at least in the initial decision in 1837, which signaled the demise of respondeat superior—the English case of *Priestley v. Fowler.* This was a doctrinal development that has inspired strong comment ever since. A critic of another doctrine, which stemmed from the decision of Judge Abinger, in *Priestly v. Fowler,* said, "Lord Abinger planted it, other judges watered it, and the Devil gave it increase."

American judges rather quickly took what had been said in *Priestley,* and wrote even stronger decisions based on it. Of those subsequent decisions, none was more important than the Massachusetts case of *Farwell v. Boston and Worchester Railway Company,* of 1842. Although legal principles usually are not remembered as being sent eastward across the

Atlantic, England borrowed from the United States in this instance. English judges picked up ideas from the Farwell case, broadened them, and made them an enduring part of English law. This, in turn, served as a cornerstone for other American decisions, including a number of them in Texas after statehood.[13]

What exceptions were judges making to the old doctrine of respondeat superior? They were arguing, for example, that an employee could not recover damages from a negligent employer after an occupational accident in the event that a "fellow servant" of the injured employee had done something that helped cause the accident. Courts began reassessing the position of co-employees within the workplace. Judges increasingly were referring to negligent co-employees not as agents of a mutual employer, but as fellow servants of the injured persons. Despite the quaint language of its originator, Lord Abinger, in the case of *Priestley v. Fowler*, the "fellow servant" rule was a provocative legal statement about the relative position of workers in regard to their employers.[14]

The fellow servant rule was an offshoot of an older rule of common law—the doctrine of common employment. The decisions stating the fellow servant rule were very well-crafted and broadly applied by judges such as Lemuel Shaw, the chief justice of the Massachusetts supreme court. The fellow servant rule, therefore, became the best-known branch of the doctrine of common employment, because it spoke to situations in which workers were employed in large-scale enterprises, such as the new railways of both England and America. The doctrine of common employment and the fellow servant rule found voice in the United States initially in the Farwell case, which involved injury to a railway worker in Massachusetts soon after railroads began to be constructed there.[15]

Besides the fellow servant rule, courts of law in the mid-nineteenth century made two other important exceptions to respondeat superior—the legal rules known as the assumption of risk doctrine, and the doctrine of contributory negligence. Judges who argued for "assumption of risk" declared that the time for employees to state their fears about workplace safety was at the moment when they were hired. Prospective workers ought to be alert enough to the possibility that they might be injured in dangerous new enterprises such as railways, that they would mention that fear to employers, as a point of negotiation about wages.[16]

Courts following the Farwell case told injured workers that they ought to have bargained with employers when they were hired, for wages high enough so that in the event that accidents did occur, the workers already would have put aside enough money to have covered their costs, out of their own savings. The doctrine of contributory negligence meant that injured employees were placed in the awkward position of showing that they themselves had in no way contributed to the accidents in which they had been injured. If they had contributed toward the accidents, they could not recover damages from their employers, even if the employers had been 90 percent to blame and they only 10 percent.[17]

This rather bleak situation was what an employee faced in the United States, after Texas joined the union, because the mid-1840s was exactly the time when the doctrine of respondeat superior was being repudiated by judges. Taken together, all of these exceptions to respondeat superior destroyed the rule itself. It became extremely difficult for most workers to recover damages from their employers, if they took a case to court. For employees in physically demanding and technologically imperfect new enterprises such as railways and steam engine operation, the judicial turning away from respondeat superior worked a particular hardship.

The law changed course again, after mid-century. Several state legislatures began passing laws, especially in the 1870s and 80s, which prohibited the full application of the common law rules of employer liability. Courts also began to rethink the status of certain "fellow employees." Certain supervisory employees legally were classified as "vice-principals"—or employees acting on behalf of an employer—rather than as mere co-workers, in the event that such a person contributed to a work place accident.[18] England, once more, served as a model for some of these exceptions, when the British Parliament passed an important law of this type in 1880.[19] Workers found that the vice-principal rule gave them a slightly greater chance of recovering damages from negligent employers, although in Texas the application of the vice-principal rule was not as widespread as in other areas.[20]

In the early twentieth century, particularly in the early 1910s, the law began to look different, once again. Both Congress and almost every state legislature, including that of Texas, passed laws that were termed "workmen's compensation acts." It is those pieces of legislation, sometimes explicitly modeled on English workmen's compensation statutes, that serve as the basis for the law as it now stands in all American states. Texas law today, for example, is grounded in the Texas Workman's Compensation Act of 1913, and an important amendment to that Act of 1917.

The difference between employer liability and workmen's compensation was subtle but crucial. The emphasis of public policy prior to the state acts of the 1910s was upon employers' responsibilities. However it had been mangled and excepted, the law prior to the 1910s in the United States (and prior to 1880 in Britain), proceeded from the fundamental assumption that an employer had a responsibility to his employees, to see to their welfare. The notion of employer liability—thus of employer responsibility—was taken out of the new terminology. The new statutes implied that workplace accidents were so prevalent that an entire system was necessary to handle the carnage. Employee accidents, it seemed to American state legislators, were an inevitable part of work. (Much the same rhetoric—about the enormous size of the problem of unemployment, thus of the necessity of state intervention—marked English debates about social welfare legislation in the early 1900s.) Workmen's compensation laws also reflected the belief that the state had a compelling interest in participating in such a system—that compensation could not be left entirely to employers and employees to manage.[21]

The state statutes were referred to as "workmen's compensation" laws, because policymakers accepted the idea that compensation was precisely what was in order. In a legal sense, "compensation" meant financial payment to replace lost wages and to help with medical expenses. What "compensation" did not mean was as important as what it did connote. The state (such as the state of Texas) was not necessarily interested in affording judicial opportunities for revenge—for instance, through punitive damages against employers. The possibility of opting out of the compensation system initially was left to employers; an employee only had the option of choosing never to work for a boss who took a position on compensation with which the employee disagreed.

The state of Texas, however, did make two tangible gestures toward employees' interests in the 1910s legislation. The families of fatally injured employees were granted several real opportunities to sue employers, whether or not the employers had been participating in the compensation system. When such wrongful death suits reached courts, the standards of care to which Texas judges held employers were relatively high—approximately those upon which English courts had insisted in the days before the 1830s, when respondeat superior was in force. Since 1913, in wrongful death suits in Texas, employers have been told that they owe to their workers duties similar to what English courts in the 1820s might have required: employers have to provide safe machinery, a safe workplace, careful and competent co-employees, rules concerning the workplace, and warnings to inexperienced employees about unforeseen hazards.[22] The Texas rules, which today not only allow wrongful death suits for employees but almost encourage them, are based on principles similar to parliamentary legislation in 1846, which directly sanctioned suits for wrongful death for the first time.

Recently there has been a flurry of legislative activity on workers' compensation in Texas. Late twentieth-century revisions, however, have left the compensation system fundamentally the same as it was in 1917. The workers' compensation law of 1989 still is a compensation law, meaning that it does not completely reimburse victims for every loss they may have suffered. The state of Texas still does not guarantee to injured employees that they will be made whole persons again. The system will not necessarily pay for a complete recovery, or offer money in recognition of emotional damage. There will be a financial payment, not because of anyone's liability, but simply because an accident has occurred.

The law of 1989 also is very different from the old rules on employer liability—and similar to the acts of 1913 and 1917—because it does not encourage the pointing of the finger of blame by employees. Only in cases of horrendous harm (when a worker dies) is the decision to undertake a lawsuit fully the province of an employee. The Worker's Compensation Act of 1989 made some changes in the operation of the law, which are shifts in emphasis, rather than changes in direction. The act of 1989 circumscribed the position of injured employees by restricting employees' choices of doctors who can treat workplace injuries, and by regulating attorneys' relationships with injured clients. Texas legislators, in other words, tinkered with certain aspects of the compensation system that were seen as too expensive, but did not move beyond the idea of compensation.[23]

In one important way, however, the law of 1989 may herald still another new era in the history of workplace accidents, because it includes a key change in legal terminology. Now the law is called "workers' compensation," rather than "workmen's compensation." The new phrase reflects the rhetoric of law finally catching up with a trend that has been evident in the workplace for a very long time—an increasing participation by women as workers. When the authors of treatises and legislation write of "workers' compensation" rather than "workmen's compensation," they are conveying that women are statistically important enough in the work force—at least among people who experience job accidents—that they should be included in the law.

Over time, how has Anglo-American law treated those people who have been injured or killed while they worked for a living? The complicated answer is that legally, the victims of workplace accidents have been in extremely different theoretical positions, from era to era. The law of workplace accidents has changed rather markedly, in only about a century and a half in Texas. Therein, of course, lies a problem for historians. How can one make sense of these twists and turns in legal rules, these doctrines and exceptions to doctrines and abrogations of exceptions?

The writers of treatises, the guides used by legal practitioners, usually provide brief summaries of the history of workplace accident law, as a part of their books and articles. Despite the expertise of such authors in describing how the law operates, their historical vision is unsatisfying because their descriptions tend to be static. Often, treatise writers describe the law as if it were a pendulum, which swings first in one direction and then in another. In a widely used set of books by Arthur Larson, for example, it appears that the law has swung back and forth when one party (such as employees) has experienced too much hardship. With respect to occupational accidents, this implies that judges and legislators make new laws out of charitable motives—that they are on the watch for injustice being done, and that they step in and change the law of workplace accidents, when any one party is disabled too greatly.[24] This is a hopeful view of law, but it is naive.

Other scholars point to judges and legislators as having less noble agendas, when they changed the law of workplace accidents. In a famous study of chief justice Lemuel Shaw of Massachusetts, Leonard Levy tries to explain why Shaw helped to steer the law away from respondeat superior. Levy believes that Shaw was acting within the legal, economic, and social spirit of his age by developing new legal doctrine while attempting to maintain the common law tradition—that is, that Shaw did not believe that he was taking a radically new tack in regard to the law. Nonetheless, Levy not only posits the effects of legal change, he regrets those effects on at least one party to accidents—workers themselves: "Since the fellow-servant rule threw the whole loss from accidents onto innocent workers, capitalism was relieved of an enormous sum that otherwise would be due as damages. The encouragement of 'infant industry' had no greater social cost."[25]

According to Levy, the Farwell case and several like it, both in Massachusetts and in other American states, reflected the concern that if railway workers were allowed too much freedom to sue their employers, then no entrepreneurs would want to make the risky investment in railways. He states, for example, that "capitalism was relieved" of the cost of injured workers, but as a legal biographer Levy stops short of saying that Shaw intentionally served the interests of employers.

Other historians studying the law of workplace accidents have been less shy about connecting law with capitalism. Morton Horwitz has been openly critical of doctrines such as the fellow servant rule, and even has assigned blame to specific lawyers and judges, for the promulgation of certain nineteenth-century legal principles. Horwitz hints broadly, for example, that the Farwell case ended in defeat for the injured railway worker because of the "intellectual impoverishment of counsel," when faced with Shaw's resolve to subsidize railways.[26]

Horwitz overstates what was occurring in the workplaces of mid-nineteenth-century England and America when he argues, for instance, that the assumption of risk doctrine "arose in an economy which already had all but eradicated traces of an earlier model of normative relations between master and servants." In most of the United States and in England in the mid-1800s—and this was certainly true in Texas, with its near majority of the work force on farms—labor historians remind us that workplaces were by no means all industrial, or tied up with steam power; most employers and employees knew each other personally.[27]

In certain very visible workplaces (such as the new railways), employment was quite impersonal; but such workplaces were the exception, rather than the rule. Were judicial decisions driven by the economy in Texas? If judges were motivated to make decisions out of a need to spur economic growth, one must examine the economy in very specific terms, to see which sectors they were promoting. Historians of Texas law and politics need to take a close look at the role of railroad companies in influencing employer liability law, especially during the boom in Texas railway construction in the 1880s. This was exactly the time when doctrinal exceptions to respondeat superior were most common in Texas courts.

Lawrence Friedman and Jack Ladinsky chronicle the complex doctrinal changes in workplace accident law in the United States. Friedman and Ladinsky argue that lawmakers tried to preserve "a certain economic balance in the community," through the application of judicial and legislative rules about workplace accidents. Among whom, or what, did the law do a balancing act? Friedman and Ladinsky discuss the motivations of several groups—businessmen, legislators, lawyers, and legal reformers—who wished to change the law.

Friedman and Ladinsky argue that employers and groups of employers (such as the powerful National Association of Manufacturers and the National Civic Federation) were in difficult straits by the early twentieth century. They recognized that employers had gotten some vital protection, in the mid-nineteenth century, in judicial rulings that shielded them from suits for occupational accidents. That had caused hardship; it not only created difficulties for employees, who could not press cases against their employers after they were permanently disabled from taking other work. Injured employees also were a burden to their families, and to their communities (which built hospitals, for instance, or otherwise provided charity for disabled persons).

Why were legislators concerned with the fate of injured employees, after for so long watching law courts deny relief? Perhaps most important was the sense, in several state legislatures, that enterprises such as interstate railways had become too powerful, too profit oriented, and too apt to take risks with not only the welfare of workers, but the safety of the public as well. Many legislators approached the problem of employer liability with the notion that employers had not pulled their weight for too long. The effort by legislatures to limit the exceptions to respondeat superior—or to make exceptions to the exceptions—was in part the result of a worsening image of the owners of enterprises. The builders of railways, for example, by the late 1800s were less likely to be thought of as financially brave entrepreneurs than as corrupt big businessmen. Historians of Texas politics note that locally owned railways in Texas had much more support in localities than those bought up by national financiers such as Jay Gould. The creation of the Texas Railroad Commission in 1891 reflected concern over outside entrepreneurship. The successful campaigns of James Hogg for attorney general in 1886 and 1888, and for governor in 1890 and 1892, had railway regulation as a key theme.

By the early twentieth century, however, employers had a compelling argument when they pointed out that they never had been made to pay for every employee accident, even while respondeat superior had been in force. In the practical sense employers also complained that they were being financially damaged by excessive jury awards when suits for employer liability went against them. Employers told state legislatures that the law of employer liability needed changing, and not only because employers were getting the worst of suits against them. Employers made a successful case to every U.S. state legislature, including that of Texas, that employer liability law needed to be altered in order that it might be more rational, and more balanced between various interests.[28]

By "rationality" employers meant that the law would help them, as business people, but not in the crude fashion with which it had been wielded in the 1840s and '50s. Employers hoped that laws related to work place accidents would allow them to predict, even in a rough fashion, what their operating costs would be, and therefore would assist in long-term business planning. Employers—both small and large-scale ones—were afraid of massive jury awards for negligence because such awards were capricious. Employers were willing to admit that occupational accidents were going to occur, and to participate, along with employees and with the state, in the process of setting aside funds, to help the victims. Thus employers were holding out to public authorities and to potential victims the hand of compromise, when they sponsored and supported the state legislation of the progressive era, which set up systems for compensating injured employees.

Legal scholars who are part of the "law and economics" movement, such as Judge Richard Posner, argue that common law defenses such as the fellow servant rule actually assisted in the prevention of accidents, during the heyday of those doctrines in the mid-nineteenth century. (Posner at times barely disguises his nostalgia for Lemuel Shaw's assumption of risk doctrine.) Posner's writings are often germane to the question of workmen's compensation, as when he describes negligence law related to railways—a crucial arena of legal and political controversy in the late nineteenth and early twentieth centuries.

Posner's conclusions—for example, his contention that "the disabled employee, in losing a limb and receiving compensation for lost future earnings, gained a surcease from long, hard, dangerous labor"—are controversial, if not combative.[29] Posner is least convincing as a social historian—for instance, when he attempts to explain the motivations of workers who asked for money from their allegedly negligent employers. He argues that employees were motivated to go to court or not, based on their prospects for a relatively high monetary award. Scholars of working class behavior, however, posit that employees undertook actions against their employers for more complex motives, such as financial need, catharsis, and the public airing of concern over unsafe conditions.

In his study of Massachusetts in Lemuel Shaw's day, Christopher Tomlins has paid attention to the judiciary as an institution that consciously sorted out the claims of not only individuals against one another, but of institutions against each other. Anglo-American judges, Tomlins argues, may not have had a preconceived vision of who should win in any given case, but they often did know who ought to prevail in the long haul. Judges held deeply rooted ideas about which institutions ought to be responsible for certain areas of public policy, and they adjusted the technicalities of the law when something got out of kilter. Tomlins sees judges such as Shaw as acting not merely out of interest in the development of railways, but from a consideration of which persons or institutions should decide claims concerning employees' welfare.[30]

Historians of labor organizations also have written about the law of workers' compensation. Writers such as Daniel Berman have noted that unions often opposed "reforms" in the law, such as the compensation legislation of the 1910s. Berman shows that labor unions were reluctant to support any legislation that was also backed by employer groups such as the National Civic Federation. In addition, unions placed more faith at that time in common law remedies for workplace accidents, and they distrusted governmental administration of a compensation system because they thought that "government was controlled by business."[31]

Berman makes a powerful case for a point that many other scholars miss—that workers have been the most consistent losers, on the occasions when the law has been changed. Labor historians such as Berman remind legal historians that an assessment of the strictness of workers' compensation law needs to include an understanding of work place conditions. In the case of Texas, such a calculation is vital because of the fact that Texas has been characterized as the most dangerous state in the union for employees. (When scholars argue that "a construction worker in Texas is more likely to die within a year than a Huntsville death row inmate," they are not arguing for more executions.)[32] Some important groups of Texas employees, including most farm workers, long were excluded from the compensation system.[33] In labeling Texas law as comparatively generous—for instance, in permitting suits for wrongful death—historians need to recall that Texas is and historically has been very hazardous to the health of its workers.

English law has been an inspiration and a parallel for Texas law, as for most American state laws, since at least the time of respondeat superior. In a complex interaction with English doctrines and the policies of other American states, the makers of Texas law have come to two important conclusions: that there is a governmental stake in the resolution of worker's compensation claims; and that compensation, rather than an assessment of liability, is what should be offered to people who have been hurt on the job.

At best, legal doctrines on workplace accidents have been hard to follow and slippery to describe, even for legal historians. On average, the law has taken account of almost everyone with an interest in workplace accident compensation, except for working people themselves. We in the United States often pat ourselves on the back for our wisdom in relying on English examples. In the case of this area of law, however, the English and Anglo-American picture from which Texans have borrowed has not always been a pretty one.

NOTES

1. Lord Atkin, in *Radcliffe v. Ribble Motor Services, Ltd.* (1939) A.C. 215.

2. D. A. Hytowitz and R. C. A. Moore, "State Workers' Compensation Systems Under Attack," 26 *Texas Trial Law* (Spring 1990), 44–45; John W. Norris, Jr., "Extra Cost of Business Here is Killing Texas," *Dallas Morning News,* January 19, 1992; Donald T. DeCarlo and Martin Minkowicz, "Worker's Compensation and Employers' Liability Law: National Developments and Trends," 25 *Tort and Insurance Law Journal* (Winter 1990), 521–30.

3. Howard Nations and John Kirkpatrick, *Texas Workers' Compensation Law* (New York: Matthew Bender, 1990). Arthur Larson, *The Law of Workmen's Compensation* (New York: Matthew Bender, 1990).

4. See, for example, Blackstone's famous comments on the responsibility of masters for the actions of their servants in William Blackstone, *Commentaries on the Laws of England* (Chicago: University of Chicago Press, 1979), vol. 1, 410–20. Blackstone, first published in 1769, discussed the relationship between masters and servants in paternalistic terms similar to those between husband and wife, parent and child, and guardian and ward. In spite of the fact that Charles B. Labatt's important treatise was entitled *Master and Servant,* in 1913, most authorities (including the writers of state and federal statutes), by the early twentieth century preferred to use the term "employer liability," as in the Federal Employers' Liability Act of 1908 (35 Sta. 65 [1908]), and the Employers' Liability Cases, heard by the Supreme Court in the same year (207 U.S. 463, 1908). The Lawlers' authoritative textbook on the subject by the mid-1930s referred to "workmen's compensation": J. John Lawler and Gail Gates Lawler, *Texas Workmen's Compensation Law* (Chicago: Cal-

laghan and Company), 1938. Nations and Kirkpatrick's 1990 treatise employs the nongender-specific form: workers' compensation. Currently, the term "employers' liability" refers to those circumstances in which recourse to judicial remedies is allowed, under the larger workers' compensation system.

5. See, generally, Albert S. Golbert and Yenny Nun, *Latin American Laws and Institutions* (New York: Praeger, 1982), 473–74; Guillermo Floris Margadant, *An Introduction to the History of Mexican Law* (Dobbs Ferry, N.Y.: Oceana Publications), 170–72; David J. Langum, *Law and Community on the Mexican California Frontier: Anglo-American Expatriates and the Clash of Legal Traditions, 1821–1846* (Norman: University of Oklahoma Press, 1987). Langum, in his study of California law, attributes an "almost total lack of personal injury lawsuits" to an "absence of injury-causing machinery" in a preindustrial era. (Langum, 123). I would argue that that scarcity of legal action had more to do with either social pressure or a lack of hope of legal redress. Work could be very dangerous, even before steam power.

6. Marvin Schultz, "Lone Star Justice: Judicial Reform and the Texas Revolution," *West Texas Historical Association Year Book* (1990), 66–76.

7. See, generally, P. W. J. Bartrip and S. B. Burman, *The Wounded Soldiers of Industry* (Oxford: Clarendon Press, 1983), 26–28.

8. The decision of Lord Abinger in *Priestley v. Fowler,* which, ironically, laid the groundwork for the judicial repudiation of respondeat superior, spoke nostalgically of a time when employers and employees got along on a more familiar (and less litigious) basis. *Priestley v. Fowler,* 3 M. and W. 1 (1837).

9. Raphael Samuel, "Workshop of the World: Steam Power and Hand Technology in mid-Victorian Britain," *History Workshop* 3 (1977): 6–72.

10. Ralph B. Campbell and Richard G. Lowe, *Wealth and Power in Antebellum Texas* (College Station: Texas A&M University Press, 1977).

11. *Cotrell v. Stocks, Parliamentary Papers, Special Reports of the Inspectors of Factories,* X (1841): 167–69. Bartrip and Burman, *Wounded Soldiers,* 26–28.

12. These exceptions to respondeat superior applied to occupations in which special circumstances—such as being at sea for long periods of time—required unusual legal relationships between employers and employees. Early twentieth-century workmen's compensation legislation, such as Texas laws in 1913 and 1917, exempted some of these same types of employees—particularly seamen—from the operation of the compensation system. Excluded employees were often covered by other legislation, however, particularly federal laws governing common carriers involved in interstate commerce. See, generally, Nations and Kirkpatrick, *Texas Workers',* 1.06.

13. Lawrence Friedman and Jack Ladinsky, "Social Change and the Law of Industrial Accidents," in *American Law and the Constitutional Order* (Cambridge: Harvard University Press, 1978), 269–82.

14. *H. and T. C. Railway Co. v. Rider,* 62 Texas 267 (1884); *M. P. Railway Co. v. Watts,* 63 Texas 549 (1885).

15. Morton J. Horwitz, *The Transformation of American Law* (Cambridge: Harvard University Press, 1977), 63–108, 160–210.

16. *T. and P Railway Co. v. Bradford,* 66 Texas 732, 2 S.W. 595 (1886).

17. *S. A. and A. P. Railway Co. v. Wallace,* 76 Texas 636; 13 S.W. 535 (1890).

18. See, for example, the chipping away at the fellow servant rule in state cases such as *Berea Stone Co. v. Kraft,* 31 Ohio St. 287, 27 *Am. Rep.* 510 (1877), and *Lamb v. Littman,* 132 N.C. 978, 44 S.E. 646 (1903).

19. Important legislation regarding employer liability was passed by Parliament not only in 1880, but 1897 and 1906.

20. *Railway v. Williams,* 75 Texas 4, 12 S.W. 835 (1889); *Young v. Hahn,* 96 Texas 99; 70 S.W. 950 (1902).

21. Lawler and Lawler, *Texas Workmen's,* 302–303. Treatise writers often emphasize the attention that lawmakers have paid to German experience in running a welfare state.

22. *General Laws of Texas,* "Workmen's Compensation Law," S.B. no. 237, chapter 103 (1917).

23. Lawler and Lawler, *Texas Workmen's,* 2–4. The rules on the circumstances under which employees can opt in or out of the system, based on employers' participation, have been revised since the early twentieth-century Texas legislation; Texas employees today have slightly greater scope for choice. I have argued, elsewhere, that the abolition of the rule that "the action dies with the person" was hardly an act of charity by Parliament, and that for the families of people killed in workplace accidents the provision of leave to sue was, at best, only a technical comfort. See Elisabeth A. Cawthon, *Worked to Death: Job Accidents and the Law in England's Railway Age,* forthcoming. William O. Ashcraft and Anita M. Alessandra, "A Review of the New Texas Workers' Compensation System," 21 *Texas Tech Law Review* (1990): 609–34.

24. Larson, *Workmen's Compensation,* passim.

25. Leonard W. Levy, *The Law of the Commonwealth and Chief Justice Shaw* (Cambridge: Harvard University Press, 1957), 321.

26. Horwitz, *Transformation,* 210.

27. Samuel, "Workshop," 6–8.

28. See, generally, Friedman and Ladinsky, "Social Change," 275–78. S. G. Reed, *A History of Texas Railroads* (Houston, 1941), 188–91; Eugene O. Porter, "Railroad Enterprise in the Republic of Texas," *Southwestern Historical Quarterly* 59:363–71.

29. Richard A. Posner, "A Theory of Negligence," I *Journal of Legal Studies* (1972), 93. Disciples of Posner have utilized econometric analysis to carry the story forward in time. Price V. Fishback, for example, bases some of his conclusions on statistics from coal-mining areas—yet, as labor historians know, coal mines are a very distinct form of workplace, and one that has little application to Texas. Fishback maintains that workers' compensation systems since the 1910s created "a large increase in the amount and likelihood of compensation," and he, like Posner, disapproves of that development. Price V. Fishback, "Liability Rules and Accident Prevention in the Workplace: Empirical Evidence from the Early Twentieth Century," XVI *Journal of Legal Studies* (June 1987), 305–28.

30. Christopher Tomlins, "A Mysterious Power: Industrial Relations and the Legal Construction of Employment Relations in Massachusetts, 1800–1850," 6 *Law and History Review* (1988), 375–438.

31. Daniel M. Berman, *Death on the Job* (New York: Monthly Review Press, 1978), 26–27.

32. Jill Williford, "Reformers' Regress? The 1991 Texas Workers' Compensation Act," 22 *St. Mary's Law Journal* (1991), 1111–45.

33. Jerry G. Bradford, "Workers' Compensation and the Farm Worker," 9 *Thurgood Marshall Law Review* (Fall 1983), 65–84.

YASUHIDE KAWASHIMA

Fence Laws on the Great Plains, 1865–1900

THE FENCING PROBLEM has long been a fundamental concern of people who live in communities where the growing of crops competes with the pasturage of livestock. At common law, owners of domestic animals were held strictly liable for their animals' trespasses. If the animal went upon lands without the permission of the landholders, the livestock owners could be held liable for all damages. This common law rule imposed upon owners a duty to keep animals off the land of another at their peril, even though they might have been entirely faultless. It did not, however, require possessors of animals to keep them on their own land at their peril, so long as they kept them off the lands of others.[1] Despite this general rule, communities in Scotland, Ireland, Wales, Cornwall, and the north and west of England, where tillage was minimal and herding was customary, frequently had local prescriptions requiring landowners to fence their close against cattle on the adjoining property.[2] At common law, however, no such liability exists.

In North America, from the beginning of English colonization, building fences was an essential part of life in agricultural communities. On each moving frontier, the settlers constantly endeavored to separate crops and livestock. The problem of fencing, in which both farmers and livestock raisers had a deep, intense interest, naturally became one of the most persistent themes in the history of the westward movement.[3]

Departing from the English common law rule, legislatures and courts in nearly all English North America imposed upon landowners a duty to fence their close against trespassing cattle. No damages were recoverable if this requirement was not met.[4] The purpose of the policy was partly to increase the meager supply of livestock by permitting cattle to wander about in order to breed faster and partly to make full use of the vast virgin forest and grassland.

In New England and much of New York and New Jersey, where township settlement and mixed husbandry prevailed, the system of common pasturage gradually emerged. During the crop growing season, common pasture was set off and fenced, and herdsmen employed by the towns supervised grazing. After harvest, however, animals were allowed to roam at large until spring planting.[5] Although the population became more dense and undistributed land became scarce in the early eighteenth century, cattle and horses were still allowed to roam freely on the town meadow and nearby beaches.[6]

In the southern colonies, where settlements were made primarily by individuals without group cooperation, the landowners' liability was more strictly observed. An early Virginia statute of 1632 provided that "every man shall enclose his ground with sufficient fences or else to plant, uppon theire owne perill."[7] Quite different from the New England practice, all southern colonies prohibited by law the fencing of any land except under actual cultivation. Thus nonlandholders commonly grazed their cattle and hogs upon the lands of others. As late as the 1830s, Virginia planters were still trying unsuccessfully to obtain legislation to permit the fencing of their whole estates or at least pastures.[8]

Throughout the colonial period, damage by cattle gave continual problems for the settlers and provoked among some the vicious response of maiming trespassing animals. Instead of complying with the requirement to construct an adequate fence, colonists would drive off wandering livestock with dogs, cut the mane from a horse to warn its owner, drive a horse into a river and force it to stay there until it tired and drowned, or corner the animal and shoot it. Landowners, who usually considered the obligation to assume the entire expense of fencing their land unfair, thus avoided the legal procedure of impounding animals and followed instead the practice of "spoiling" them.[9]

Many planters and farmers did go to court to recover damages. When the landowner sued for damages suffered from trespass by cattle but failed to meet the standards prescribed by the colonial statute of fencing his property properly, he could not recover damages. The burden of proof was on the defendant, however, to show that the plaintiff's lands were not adequately fenced. Those who successfully rebutted the allegations of defective fences and established tangible losses would receive an award of exemplary damages.[10] The policy of keeping animals out of the fields persisted. Subsequent fencing laws drastically improved the old ones by specifying in detail requirements for sufficient fences and by imposing heavy fines on fence viewers for the neglect of their responsibilities.[11]

The great plains, although it presented an entirely different environment from that of the eastern states,[12] did undergo a similar experience. One after another, the plains states confirmed the rule of fencing that had come to characterize all earlier frontiers of British North America—fence law requiring crop husbandmen to fence out domestic animals, which were allowed to run at large without liability. However, as environmental constraints on fencing became evident, and as crop husbandmen came to predominate, they compelled the adoption of herd laws, freeing them of the obligation to fence and imposing liability on the owners of animals at large. Thus animal liability laws on the great plains reverted to principles established in English common law. This essay attempts to explain the nature of fence laws of the great plains states, dealing mainly with the eastern tier of the region.

An examination of early laws of these states clearly reveals that the common law practice of fencing in the animals had never been accepted in the area. In Kansas, the first territorial legislature enacted a law in 1855, "An Act regulating Inclosures." It imposed a duty upon landowners to fence "all fields and inclosures," specifying how a lawful fence must be constructed.[13] "If any horse, cattle or other stock shall break into any inclosure" protected by a legal fence, the owner of the livestock was to pay the injured party for the first trespass the true value of the damage, for the second offense double damages, and for any subsequent trespass treble damages together with a lien on the animal until the damages, the cost of maintenance trebled, and the rest of the suit were paid. Unless his land was enclosed by a lawful fence, the landowner could not recover for a trespass of animals negligently or even willfully caused.

This law certainly reflects the situation in the mid-nineteenth century in Kansas, which was definitely an "open range" country. The wide prairies could be used most productively for cattle grazing, and it was clearly absurd to impose upon stock owners the common law duty to keep their stock on their own land at their peril.[14] Although the act did not indicate whether the injured party could recover if the fence was not sufficient, the Kansas supreme court held in 1869 that it "probably so modified the common law that no action lies for injuries done to real estate by trespassing cattle unless such real estate is enclosed with a lawful fence."[15] In *Larkin v. Taylor* (1870), the same court ruled that the state fence law made the party having an insufficient fence liable for negligence and therefore unable to recover for injuries done to his crops by stock running at large and roaming upon his land. Nor could he recover even if the stock owner was negligent, unless it amounted to a "wilful, wanton, or malicious want of care."[16] The fence law of 1855, though modified over the years, retained its basic tenets for more than a century.

In Nebraska, the territorial legislature stipulated in 1857 that a person with a lawful fence could recover for the damage caused by animals that broke into the enclosure. An 1860 law declared that the cultivators who planted crops without enclosing the fields with a sufficient fence were liable for all damages caused by the invading animal. Subsequent laws of 1866 and 1867 repeated the provisions of the earlier laws, requiring landowners to fence their lands, and set forth various standards for lawful fences.[17]

In Texas, the tradition of open range cattle herding was introduced from the Carolinas through the upper south by the 1820s and was flourishing in northeast Texas by the 1830s.[18] As early as 1840, "An Act defining Lawful Enclosures, and for Other Purposes" was passed, requiring gardeners, farmers, and planters to build sufficient fences to prevent cattle and hogs from passing through the enclosures. Complaints could be heard before the justice of the peace, who would appoint two "disinterested and impartial freeholders" to examine the condition of the fence and the damage sustained. If the owner of land with an insufficient fence "maim, wound, or kill" any invading stock, he was to make full satisfaction to the injured person.[19]

After 1848, the herding system came to be modified by Hispanic contacts, and the Hispanicized open range cattle ranching continued to thrive in Texas.[20] Another fence law passed in 1879 substantially repeated the 1840 law, with a new provision giving the landowner the power to impound livestock that invaded his land for a second time.[21]

Montana passed a law in the early 1870s making a lawful fence entirely surrounding the grounds a prerequisite for the plaintiff to bring a successful action for damages against the owner of trespassing animals. The owner of unenclosed lands could not recover for the destruction of the grass caused by straying sheep unless they were maliciously driven upon the lands for the purpose of causing injury.[22]

In Wyoming, the laws of 1876, 1887, and 1899 affirmed the rule established earlier in the eastern great plains states, by recognizing the animal owners' right to permit them to run at large and requiring landowners to fence out the animals. But these laws made individuals owning horses, mules, or cattle which breached into any lawful enclosure liable for all damages sustained.[23]

South Dakota statutes of 1877, 1883, and 1887 made any person liable for the trespasses by his horses, mules, and cattle as long as the land was legally fenced in.[24] In North Dakota, the construction and the maintenance of a legal fence to prevent trespass by cattle was the custom from the very beginning. The statutes of 1895 and 1899 stipulated that any person owning livestock that went through, over, or under any lawful fence would be liable for all resulting damages. The person suffering damages by livestock trespass could take up the offending animal, but was required to notify the owner of this seizure without unnecessary delay.[25] Colorado passed an act in 1855 giving any person who maintained a lawful fence in good repair the right to recover damages for trespass and injury to grass, garden or vegetable products, or other crops from the owner of any livestock that broke through the fence.[26]

Oklahoma approached the problem in a different way. In 1890, when the territory of Oklahoma was organized, a law was passed, which was reenacted in 1893, stating that the owners of "swine, sheep, goats, stallions and jacks" should restrain them from running at large. All other stock should also be restrained unless permitted to run at large in an express prescription. On a petition signed by twenty-five freeholders, the county commissioners would divide their county into districts for the purpose of determining whether the stock not enumerated would be allowed to roam freely. If the commissioners found a district suitable, the residents of the district could present the board of county commissioners a petition, signed by one-fourth of the voters, to have their stock run at large during the night or certain months of the year. In such a district, the landowners had to enclose their land with sufficient fences.[27]

Did the owner of public land, the U.S. government, have the obligation to adhere to the "fence-out" rule prevailing in most of the great plains states? The government's policy seemed to confirm the idea of open range and apply it fully where farmers were not present. In *Buford v. Houtz* (1890), the U.S. supreme court spoke of an implied license, growing out of the hundred-year-old custom that federal lands should be free to the people who sought to use them, where they were left open and unenclosed, and no act of government could forbid that use.[28] In banning the fencing of public land, a federal circuit court, in a Montana case in 1908, held that the United States had the unlimited right to control the occupation of the public lands, and that no state could require fencing of their lands.[29]

Accordingly, the Forest Service and the Bureau of Land Management drew up regulations prohibiting unlicensed livestock from grazing on lands under the control of these agencies and provided impoundment and damage procedures against the owners of trespassing livestock.[30] In *Light v. U.S.* (1911), the supreme court sanctioned the action of local forest officials who had barred a Colorado rancher from the land after his stock had been turned loose near a national forest boundary. It also held that fence laws did not authorize wanton and willful trespass, nor did they afford immunity to those who, in disregard of property rights, turned loose their cattle under circumstances showing that they intended to graze these animals upon another's land. The court, however, found it unnecessary to establish guidelines concerning how far the U.S. government was required to fence public land.[31]

The farmers on the great plains, who were subject to the fence law, could not meet its requirement to fence their lands effectively because of lack of timber. Nor could they raise crops if cattle were allowed to roam freely. Moreover, there were many abuses and violations of the fence law, often harmful to the farmers. Fence laws were designed to permit stock to run at large and graze on the plains and to relieve the owners from an action for damages by livestock wandering upon land unprotected by a lawful fence. These laws neither specifically stated nor necessarily implied that there could be no recovery without a lawful fence. But the court, in *Larkin v. Taylor* (1870), held that a landowner had a right to recover damages if the trespass was "wilful or wanton." The court reasoned that the act imposed a positive duty upon the landowner to fence; therefore, it was negligence to fail to fence lawfully. Yet the landowner could recover damages if the animal owner was guilty of some degree of fault worse than negligence—wanton or willful trespass.[32]

"Wilful or wanton trespass" was at times difficult to define. In a Wyoming case, the mere turning loose of stock upon one's own premises or upon the public domain was declared not to constitute in itself a willful or intentional trespass, notwithstanding that the owner knew the stock might stray to another's land.[33] In a Texas case, *Moore v. Pierson* (1906), the defendant was held not liable unless he "knew and intended" that his cattle would break through the plaintiff's fence. In another Texas case, the defendant was found not to have committed willful trespass because he did not know that his cattle were vicious or were likely to communicate disease to the plaintiff's stock.[34]

On the other hand, the defendant's overstocking was found to be willful trespass in *Lazarus v. Phelps* (1894) when a deliberate intent to obtain the benefit of another's pasturage was shown. The court stated that the Texas statute (requiring lands under cultivation to be fenced and providing that if a fence should be insufficient the stock owner would not be made liable for resulting damage) "could never have been intended . . . to authorize the cattle deliberately to take possession of such land and depasture their cattle upon them without making compensation."[35]

But ten years later the Wyoming supreme court ruled that a defendant who had turned out more cattle upon his own land than it could reasonably support was held not liable for damages caused by his cattle wandering upon and dispasturing the plaintiff's unenclosed premises. It found that willfulness in the overstocking of his land could not be proven.[36]

In the states where fence laws were enacted, it was recognized that the driving of stock onto another's land for purposes of pasturing or watering constituted willful or intentional trespass. Thus, the Idaho court, in *Swanson v. Groat* (1906), held that a person who willfully and deliberately drove his stock upon the land of another, whether enclosed or unenclosed, and herded and grazed them upon the land over the owner's "protest and objections" was liable for the trespass. "Such wilful, deliberate, and intentional conduct," the court asserted, "cannot be justified upon the theory that the stock had a right of their own accord to roam over and graze upon such land."[37] In *Jones v. Blythe* (1908), the Utah court held the defendant liable for intentionally driving his sheep upon the plaintiff's land. The court distinguished between the straying of animals onto the land (unintentional) and the driving of such animals onto the land (willful).[38]

It was held, in *Wilson v. Caffall* (1904), that there was no trespass under the laws of Texas where goats and other animals turned out daily on certain land and then went through an insufficient fence to the plaintiff's pasture. The Wyoming court, in *Hardman v. King* (1906), while recognizing the herding of cattle on another's land as an actionable trespass, stated that if the cattle had strayed to such land and were subsequently being driven from there, that conduct would not constitute an actionable trespass for which recovery could be held.[39] A Colorado case, *Bell v. Gonzales* (1905), established the rule that the fence statute did not apply to cases where cattle owners deliberately took possession of the land, trespassing upon and pasturing their cattle under such circumstances as to show a deliberate intent to obtain the benefit of another's pasturage.[40]

As some distressed colonists did earlier, aggrieved farmers on the plains occasionally resorted to self-help, by wounding and killing the stock that intruded onto their lands. The Texas fence law of 1840 warned that the landowner must make full restitution to the livestock owner for maiming, wounding, or killing offending horses, cattle, or hogs. In 1851, the Texas court held, in *Cole v. Tucker,* that the act of 1840 defining lawful enclosure did not limit the damages merely to compensation, but could include exemplary or vindictive damages where the circumstances justified them. Seven years later, the same court held, in *Champion v. Vincent* (1858), that where the defendant, whose fence was not a lawful one, shot the plaintiff's hogs, which were in defendant's potato patch, the act was committed deliberately, in willful violation of the plaintiff's rights. The court pointed out that the defendant deliberately took his pistol and shot the hogs down, instead of putting up a fence to protect his crop. The law, therefore, allowed damages beyond the strict measure of compensation, by way of punishment and for example's sake.[41] The Kansas law of 1855 imposed double damages and costs on anyone who wounded or killed livestock that invaded his land not enclosed by a legal fence.[42]

The fence law prevailing on the great plains, which guaranteed the open range policy by forcing landowners to enclose their fields, came to be counterbalanced by the herd laws. The Kansas territorial statutes of 1855 included a provision that anticipated the herd laws. "An Act respecting Seed Horses" declared: "If any seed horse, mule, or jackass, over the age of two years, be found running at large, the owner shall be fined five dollars for the first offense and not exceeding ten dollars for every subsequent offense." If these animals kept for breeding and training purposes escaped by carelessness, the owner would not only be liable for all the damages sustained but also be fined three dollars for the first offense and ten dollars for every subsequent offense.[43] In contrast with the fence law, which was mainly designed for preventing trespass by animals, this law aimed at the protection of female animals and, therefore, applied only to male animals old enough to harm a female.[44]

The early fence laws adopted by Kansas and Nebraska were perfectly acceptable to the farmers as long as they remained in the eastern parts of the states, where timber was plentiful. Even when they did not have enough fence materials, farmers, who were usually working in the field nearby, could easily drive the intruding animals away during the day, though they still needed protection at night.[45] To solve the problem, the legislatures passed night herd laws. Nebraska in the 1860s passed a series of laws ordering the confinement of livestock at night in various counties, usually during the growing season.[46] In 1868, Kansas farmers were also able to secure the "night herd law," which gave the electors of each township the power to decide whether the "fence-out" or "fence-in" policy should be enforced in their township during the night. The fence law ruled the daylight hours, but a majority of the township electors could, by petitioning the county board, require the owners of domestic animals to confine them at night during specified portions of the year.[47] Later, the court ruled that the order could specify the entire year if the people so desired.[48]

As more farmers settled in the western parts of the states, they felt the need for more general herd laws in order to prevent cattle from invading their fields. For these farmers, who had either only inadequate fencing or none at all, these cattle were indefensible. The efforts of the legislatures in trying to accommodate the farmers by making any possible material a legal fence clearly demonstrate the difficulties the farmers were in.[49] In the western and frontier counties of Kansas and Nebraska, where little timber was available, the fence law was an absurdity for the farmers. Board fences were too expensive, and hedges of osage orange, although effective, took time to grow to form fencing. Thus the herd law, which would oblige livestock owners to control their animals and would relieve the farmers from the task of fence building, was a vital necessity.[50]

Farmers in some localities had in addition some specific reasons to advocate the herd law. Kansas farmers in Ellsworth County, for example, thought a herd law would eliminate the obnoxious practice of "wintering" Texas cattle. These cattle, which were bought cheaply in the fall, often invaded and depredated farmers' fields, while turned loose to forage for themselves until they could be sold at higher prices in the spring.[51] Many Kansans considered Texas drovers the most persistent offenders in farm devastation and advocated a crippling of the cattle trade through a rigorous enforcement of herd laws. Farmers were disgusted not only with the Texas cowboys' negligence in letting their longhorns trample the fields, but also their orneriness in deliberately driving herds into the meadows. Successful implementation of herd laws would certainly end the long drive of Texas longhorns to Kansas and the splenic fever carried by them.[52]

The herd laws were usually the result of the long struggle of crop farmers, who favored the strict liability principle of the common law, against stock raisers, who held on to the "open range" policy embodied in the fence law. The general herd laws pertained to most stock animals and limited the privilege of allowing them to run at large. The laws aimed at requiring the owners or keepers to restrain certain animals under some circumstances and provided remedies for the breach of this duty. These laws, therefore, constituted a deviation from the "open range" policy, which was embodied in the fence law, but a step toward the common law policy.

In Nebraska, general herd law proposals went down to defeat in the legislature twice before their finally being adopted in 1871. The county option herd law enacted in 1888 had the effect of transforming the Nebraska panhandle. The farmers quickly created ten counties out of the two counties as a means of outvoting the ranchers and of opting for county-based herd laws, thereby ending the open range.[53]

Kansas passed herd laws for specific counties and townships, for Crawford in 1870 and for twelve other counties by the end of 1871. These laws, however, were inconsistent: the legislature required a vote in some counties, permitted a petition in others, and denied a vote in the rest. In 1871, the Kansas supreme court declared, in *Darling v. Rodgers,* the herd laws of 1870 and 1871 unconstitutional because they were contrary to the equal treatment of counties guaranteed by the state constitution.[54] The legislature accordingly passed a new herd law in February 1872, establishing the county option and empowering the county commissioners with the authority to decide on the herd law. Among the seventy-two counties that had been established by the end of 1872, twenty-six counties enforced the herd law. Dickinson County, as one of the first counties to call it into force, contributed to the decline of Abilene as a cow town.[55]

Two years later, a new herd law was adopted, giving the county board the power to determine which animals should be allowed to roam freely. It also stipulated that two-thirds of the voters could petition the county commissioners to adopt the herd law and that a majority of the voters could petition to nullify the law.[56] Although only one county rescinded the herd law, it was not until 1889 that the general herd law applicable to all the counties passed, requiring all animals of a certain age (usually the males above the age of one year and females above two years) to be fenced in. This statute became the basis for the Herd Law of 1929, which was applicable to all livestock throughout the state.[57]

The long struggle between the advocates of the fence law and herd law provoked much litigation. These law suits involved farmer against farmer as well as farmer against cattle raiser. In *Wellis v. Beal* (1870), the defendant's hogs broke through a fence into an inclosure and destroyed a crop. The court held that the insufficiency of the fence was no defense against the plaintiff's claim for damages. It pointed out that hogs were allowed to run at large in a township where the hog law had been suspended by vote of the people. The hog law reenacted the common law requiring every man not to let his own stock roam freely, except at his own peril, but it gave each township the right, by a vote, to suspend the law. The court, ruling in favor of the plaintiff, stated that the fence law authorized cattle to roam at large, but this implication could not outweigh the express prohibition by another statute.[58]

Railroads became the center of controversy when a new amendment was added to the fence law in 1874, requiring the companies to fence off their tracks to avoid killing stock. In *Central Branch Railroad Co. v. Lea* (1878), the Kansas supreme court held that a stockman could not collect damages for an animal killed by a train, because both had been in violation of the law.[59] In *Atchison, Topeka, and Santa Fe v. Yates* (1879), the court found the defendant railroad not liable for two hogs killed in a county where the herd law for hogs was not adopted, because the existing fence law did not require the building of hog-proof fences. In 1884, the court, in two cases—*Atchison, Topeka, and Santa Fe v. Riggs* and *A., T., and S.F. v. Howard*—held that when the stockman did obey the herd law but the railroad did not obey the fence law, the stockman could recover damages from the railroad.[60]

In *Leavenworth, Topeka, and Southwestern Railway Co. v. Forbes* (1887), the court ruled that the railroads did not need to fence at all in the herd law country. This decision, however, was overturned by *Missouri Pacific Railway Co. v. Baxter* (1891). Baxter, a sheep owner in Dickinson County, brought suit for his sheep killed by a Missouri Pacific train. The railroad argued that it had not built fences in the county because the county had a herd law and fences would not have kept sheep off the tracks. The supreme court supported Baxter's arguments and, thus, upheld the 1874 statute that required railroads to build fences.[61]

In Texas, when the state legislature passed a law in 1870 providing for settlement by local option (by the vote of fifty freeholders of a county or twenty freeholders of a subdivision of the county), the eastern part of the state promptly adopted a law requiring people to fence their stock, while west Texas clung to the open range system.[62]

The Oklahoma law of 1890 that reintroduced the fence-in rule of the common law, requiring every owner of swine, sheep, goats, stallions, jacks, and all other stock to restrain them from running at large throughout the year, seems to reflect the general condition of the great plains at the end of the nineteenth century, where the herd law became the rule over the fence law. The privilege previously bestowed by the fence law in the other states became only an option. The county commissioners were given the power, on a petition signed by twenty-five freeholders of the township or district, to divide their counties into districts to determine in which districts stock other than swine, sheep, goats, stallions, and jacks should be permitted to run at large. One-fourth of the legal voters in a selected district could decide to have stock run at large for the entire year, certain months, or just during the daytime.[63] A 1903 law required landowners to construct partition fences in districts where stock were allowed to run at large from sunrise to sundown or during certain months in the year. The neighbors were to share equally the expense of the construction and maintenance of the fences.[64]

The county herd law had been modified from time to time, but the basic policy of county option prevailed until the 1920s, when the legislatures enacted laws of statewide application. A Kansas act of 1929, for example, made it unlawful for any neat cattle, horses, mules, asses, swine, or sheep to run at large, made the animal owners liable to the injured persons, and allowed those harmed to have a lien on the invading animals.[65] This law abandoned the principles of township and county option embodied in the night herd law and the county herd law. It was a rejection of the policy of the fence law and was, in turn, a clear affirmation of the common law rule.

Ironically, the herd law developed on the great plains in the 1870s and 80s came to influence agricultural practice in the south, where fencing crops in and animals out was standard from colonial times. In the postbellum period, the open range came to be severely restricted and eventually ceased to exist. It was during the 1880s and 90s that such states as Georgia, Mississippi, and Alabama began to restrict the movement of stock and continued to do so until 1903, when they finally established statewide laws.[66]

Herd law was also significant in initiating a trend that was accelerated by barbed wire. Barbed wire, which was developed by Joseph F. Glidden of Illinois and other inventors in the 1870s, made fencing inexpensive and revolutionized fencing on the great plains. It not only necessitated a change in the original requirements for lawful fence, but also brought about profound changes in farming and ranching, including the disappearance of the open, free range, the emergence of fenced pastures and stock farming, and the founding of more profitable small farms. As both farmers and stock raisers found it to their advantage to enclose, crops and livestock could coexist through the use of fields as pasture.[67] Many of the benefits claimed to have been brought about by barbed wire, however, had already been provided by herd law. Although little fence was built on the great plains before barbed wire, small farmers were well established. Thanks to the herd law, they could not only avoid expensive fence building but also prevent livestock from invading their fields.[68]

The advent of barbed wire led to various violations of the fence law. Before barbed wire it was not possible to fence large areas, but now cattlemen could fence vast areas, sometimes enclosing areas they did not own—government land, the land of homestead farmers, and leased land—as well as their own land. For example, the "Cherokee Strip" in the Indian Territory, across the Kansas state line, in the early 1870s became an important area for grazing Texas trail herds. By the mid-1870s numerous cattlemen had informally preempted large sections of the strip. By the early 1880s some large ranchers began enclosing with cheap barbed wire not only their own ranches but some nearby small ranges despite the strong protests by the owners.[69]

Abuses resulting from the extensive fencing practice led to the enactment of a series of laws designed to eliminate them.[70] In Texas, for example, an act of 1884 required the construction of a gateway in every three miles of fencing, and another act prohibited the unlawful fencing of small landowners' property and of the public school, university, and asylum lands.[71]

At times, violations of the law provoked retaliations in the form of fence-cutting. This practice was prevalent in Texas, Wyoming, and New

Mexico, where strong animosity developed between fence men (graziers) and no-fence men (cowboys and small cowmen). Small cowmen needed free range, which was increasingly appropriated by the fence men, and decided to resort to cutting fence.[72] In some plains states fence-cutting was made a felony punishable by imprisonment. A Texas law of 1884 stipulated a prison term of one to five years for anyone who would wantonly and willfully cut or destroy any fence. This law recognized the reality that fences were being continuously destroyed in many parts of the state by lawless persons and that the existing penalty was not sufficient to deter offenders and suppress the crime.[73]

In *Fugate v. Smith* (1894), the Colorado supreme court affirmed a judgment against the defendant and held that the Colorado fence statute had no applicability in an action for trespass by the defendant's stock upon the plaintiff's land, where the fence was willfully broken by the defendant himself, claiming that the fence was on his land. The defendant was declared to be a trespasser and liable for the consequent injury, no matter what the character of the fence.[74] In another Colorado case, *Norton v. Young* (1895), an action for damages by trespass by sheep, the defense of absence of a lawful fence was rejected, when it was proven that the sheep did not break through but that the fence had been cut and torn down by the defendant deliberately for the purpose of pasturage.[75] An Oklahoma law of 1893 imposed imprisonment not exceeding four years on persons who would willfully burn the fences of others.[76]

Availability of inexpensive barbed wire also had a detrimental effect on federal public land, which had been left open and unenclosed for the people who wanted to use it. The first users on much of the federal land were graziers. Conflicts developed when they started fencing the public lands for their own uses.[77] The problem became very acute in some plains states like Wyoming, where federal lands comprised more than half the surface area.

In 1885, congress passed "An Act to Prevent the Unlawful Occupancy of the Public Lands," making it illegal for a person to erect or maintain an inclosure around or to assert the exclusive use of any public land. This was based upon the federal policy not only to dispose of the vacant public lands but also to allow free grazing on the open range of the public domain.[78] Since the fencing out of settlers clearly conflicted with national policy, the act gave potential settlers a legal remedy for being excluded from the public domain. Moreover, the government had a duty to prosecute those who were monopolizing the range, and it did so on many occasions.[79]

The public's right to access to unfenced public lands came to be fully recognized by the Supreme Court in *Buford v. Houtz* (1890). The plaintiffs, cattle graziers, sought to enjoin sheep-raisers from bringing their herds onto the area. The court saw no equity in barring the sheepmen from the public land and upheld the denial of an injunction.[80] In *Camfield v. U.S.* (1897), the defendants erected a fence around two townships of checkerboard land (46,000 acres). Upon prosecution for violating the Unlawful Occupancy Act of 1885, the defendants asserted that it was unconstitutional for the government to enjoin fences that were located not on public land but on private property. The Supreme Court, however, found that the fence did interfere with legitimate uses of public land and ruled that the government action was an appropriate use of police power. The court conceded that a landowner had the right to protect interests on private property with fences.

If, however, under the guise of enclosing his own land, one built a fence that was useless for that purpose but was only intended to enclose government lands, he was guilty, the court insisted, of an unwarrantable appropriation of the right belonging to the public at large.[81]

The Taylor Grazing Act of 1934 virtually ended the disputes over unfenced public lands. The federal government withdrew public lands from entry to homesteaders, eliminating the competition between settlers and graziers. The act also changed the grazing on public land from a commons to a permit system regulated by the government. Those persons who were grazing stock in 1934 were given a right to use the public lands to the exclusion of others, thus doing away with the competition for public grazing land among the graziers.[82]

The evolution of fence law on the great plains during the second half of the nineteenth century parallels the settlement process of the region. On America's last frontier, the policy of "fence-out" was the standard rule from the beginning of settlement, and cattle and horses were allowed to roam freely on the open range. This policy came to be fully written into law in all the plains states except Oklahoma.

As time went on, several developments began gradually to undermine this basic policy. Barbed wire, which made fencing inexpensive, brought about the possibility of extensive fencing by graziers and farmers, and they soon converted the open range into well-fenced pastures and farms on the plains. Some of the graziers even started to fence government land for their own use, excluding the public that had the right to utilize it. This abuse led to legislation aimed at restricting grazing on federal land. This eventually resulted in the complete elimination of free range on the public land by the early twentieth century.

Above all, the open range policy supported by the fence law came to be seriously challenged by a series of herd laws, which successively established a township option policy and a county option policy. That policy was finally abolished on a statewide basis by the end of the 1920s. These herd laws, which imposed on stock owners a duty to restrain animals, frustrating the traditional American fence law, contributed to the transformation of the great plains into a "fence-in" country, as set forth in the common law. The trend was clearly evident at the turn of the nineteenth century. The decline of the open range and return to the English common law rule of fencing marked the end of the frontier on the great plains.

NOTES

1. William Prosser, *Handbook of the Law of Torts* (2nd. ed., 1955), 319–20; Richard B. Morris, *Studies in the History of American Law* (2nd. ed., 1964), 208–9; Casad, "The Kansas Law of Livestock Trespass: A Study in Statutory Underpainting," 10 *Kansas Law Review* 56 (1961).

2. Morris, *Studies,* 209; McWhiney and McDonald, "Celtic Origins of Southern Herding Practices," 51 *Journal of Southern History* (1985), 165–82.

3. The fence problem has long attracted scholarly attention. Two brief but succinct overviews of fencing in colonial America are Morris, *Studies,* 208–35; and Forrest MacDonald, *Novus Ordo Seclorum: The Intellectual Origins of the Constitution* (1985), 29–31. The New England fencing practice has been discussed in such general works as William Weeden, *Economic and Social History of New England, 1620–1789* (1890), 58–67, 275–78, 404–405; Percy Bidwell and John Falconer, *History of Agriculture in the Northern United States, 1620–1860* (1925), 21–25, 55–58; Sumner Powell, *Puritan Village: The Formation of a New England Town* (1963), 14, 19, 122, 141–42, 184–85; Howard Russell, *A Long, Deep Furrow: Three Centuries of Farming in New England* (1976), 35–37, 40–63, 73–74, 79, 126–27, 155; and David Allen, *In English Ways: The Movement of Societies and the Transferal of English Local Law and Custom to Massachusetts Bay in the Seventeenth Century* (1982), 46–47, 49–50.

Scholars have paid closer attention to the colonial south and the antebellum south, where the open range prevailed. Lewis Gray argues that the open range was a home-grown necessity in the south, which had a great expanse of land but small cultivated areas, so crops were fenced in in preference to closing the range. Lewis Gray, *History of Agriculture in the Southern United States to 1860* (1933), I, 138–51, II, 843. This view has been confirmed by a number of other scholars, including Terry Jordan, whose *Trails to Texas: Southern Roots of Western Cattle Ranching* (1981) provides an excellent account of how open range cattle raising moved steadily from the seventeenth-century Carolinas to the Texas of the 1870s.

On the other hand, Forrest McDonald and Grady McWhiney maintain that the open range was not a mere creation of the southern physical environment, but was itself a tradition for the people of Celtic heritage who settled the southern region. See Forrest McDonald and Grady McWhiney, "The Antebellum Southern Herdsman: A Reinterpretation," 41 *Journal of Southern History* (1975), 147–66; "The South from Self-Sufficiency to Peonage: An Interpretation," 85 *American Historical Review* (1980), 1095–1118, and "Celtic Origins of Southern Herding Practices," 51 *Journal of Southern History* (1985), 165–82.

One of the significant works done on the southern open range is J. Crawford King, Jr., "The Closing of the Southern Range: An Exploratory Study," 48 *Journal of Southern History* (1982), 53–70. King explains why the policy of fencing crops in and animals out persisted, despite the repeated protests of planters, until long after the Civil War, and argues that the end of the open range was a part of a profound set of changes that reshaped the social, economic, and political life of the region. This is a very suggestive interpretation that could be useful in understanding the transformation of the fencing policies on the great plains, which took place in a shorter duration.

Perhaps the most dramatic phase of the history of fencing in the United States was that of the great plains after the Civil War, which is vividly told in Walter Prescott Webb, *The Great Plains* (1931), 280–318. Although some of his views came to be challenged by later historians, Webb provided a sound basic framework in which the fencing problem could be comprehended.

Earl Hayter, in his "Livestock-Fencing Conflict in Rural America," 37 *Agricultural History* (1963), 10–20, presents a general but valuable survey of problems resulting from insufficient fencing that were all too common to rural areas in the United States. His larger work, *The Troubled Farmer, 1850–1900: Rural Adjustment to Industrialism* (1968), treats the fence problem within the context of the personal and technical aspects of the farmer's daily life during the period following the Civil War. Similarly, Robert Dykstra, in his *The Cattle Towns* (1968), demonstrates that herd laws are related to the long drive of Texas longhorns to Kansas, and the splenic fever carried by these animals.

Recently a number of useful studies, concentrating mainly on Kansas and Nebraska, have been done, with a narrower focus on specific aspects or periods. See, for example, the works of Rodney Davis, Jan Farrar, Earl Hayter, Leslie Hewes, Alvin Peters, and Charles Wood. Taken together, these works present an overall picture of the problems relating to fences and fencing, but a need still exists for a more comprehensive treatment of the subject on the great plains, especially its legal aspect.

4. *Records of the Governor and Company of the Massachusetts Bay in New England, 1628–1686,* Nathaniel Shurtleff, ed. (1953–54), II:106, 215, 332, I:15, 15, 39, III:241; *The Colonial Laws of Massachusetts, 1660–1672,* William Whitmore, ed. (1889), 132; Morris, *Studies,* 209.

5. Weeden, *History,* 58–67, 275–78, 404–405; Bidwell and Falconer, *History,* 21–25, 55–58; Allen, *English Ways,* 46–47, 49–50; Morris, *Studies,* 210; McWhiney and McDonald, "Celtic Origins," 170; McDonald, *Novus Ordo Seclorum,* 30.

6. 2 *Acts and Resolves, Public and Private, of the Province of Massachusetts Bay* (1869–1922) [hereafter *Mass. Acts and Resolves*]; 4 id. 426–28; 1 *Laws of New York from 1691–1772,* 373–74; 3 *Laws of New Hampshire* (1679–1835) (1902–22), 128.

7. 1 *The Statutes at Large; Being a Collection of All the Laws of Virginia, 1619–1792,* William W. Hening, ed. (1809–23), 176–99. For a similar Maryland statute of 1640, see

1 *Maryland Archives* 96. The Virginia statute of 1632, however, was not adopted without opposition. The opponents urged that the act would encourage the owners of swine to dispense with keepers and would result in livestock committing trespasses unchecked upon private property. Accordingly, the fence law was modified in 1639, requiring owners to confine their swine securely in pens at night and to provide keepers for them during the day. But in 1642 the original rule concerning swine was restored. 1 *The Statutes-at-Large,* 228, 244.

8. Gray, *History,* I:138–51, II:843; McDonald and McWhiney, "Herdsman," 147–66; McDonald and McWhiney, "South," 1105–11; King, "Closing," 53–70; Jordan, *Trails,* 1–58; McDonald, *Novus Ordo Seclorum,* 30–31.

9. *The Colonial Laws of Massachusetts, 1672–1686,* William Whitmore, ed. (1887), 124–25; David Konig, *Law and Society in Puritan Massachusetts, 1629–1692* (1979), 144.

10. Morris, *Studies,* 211–15; Yasuhide Kawashima, *Puritan Justice and the Indian: White Man's Law in Massachusetts, 1630–1763* (1986), 63.

11. 1 *Mass. Acts and Resolves,* 333–34; Konig, *Law,* 187.

12. Webb, *Great Plains,* 281–82

13. *Kansas Territorial Statutes* (1855), chap. 83.

14. Casad, "Kansas Law," 58.

15. *Union Pacific Railway v. Rollins,* 5 *Kansas* 1677 (1869), 177.

16. 5 *Kansas* 260.

17. *Laws of Nebraska* (1857), 370–71; *Laws of Nebraska* (1860), 645–46; *Nebraska Territorial Laws* (1867), chap. 1, 17, chap. 2, 17, chap. 3.

18. Jordan, *Trails,* 101–102.

19. *Paschal's Digest* (1866), articles 3838–40.

20. For the Spanish ranching tradition, see Sandra Myres, "The Spanish Cattle Kingdom in the Province of Texas," 4 *Texana* 233–46; *The Ranch in Spanish Texas, 1691–1800* (1969); and "The Ranching Frontier: Spanish Institutional Backgrounds of the Plains Cattle Industry," in *Essays on the American West,* Harold Hollingsworth and Sandra Myres, eds. (1969), 19–39.

21. *General Laws of Texas* (1879), articles 2431–35.

22. *Smith v. Williams,* 2 *Montana* 195 (1874); *Faut v. Lyman,* 9 *Montana* 61, 22 *Pacific* 120 (1889); *Bernhorn v. Griswald,* 27 *Montana* 79, 69 *Pacific* 557 (1902).

23. *Wyoming Compiled Laws* (1876), chap. 51, articles 3, 5 to 8; *Revised Statutes* (1887), articles 4185, 4187 to 4190; *Revised Statutes* (1899), articles 1976 to 1989; *Hecht v. Harrison,* 5 *Wyoming* 279, 40 *Pacific* 306 (1895); *Garretson v. Avery,* 26 *Wyoming* 53, 176 *Pacific* 433 (1918).

24. *South Dakota C. Civil P.* (1877), article 747; *Special Laws* (1883), chap. 115, article 1; *Special Laws* (1885), chap. 17, articles 4, 5; *Civil Laws* (1887), article 750.

25. *North Dakota C. Civil P.* (1877), article 750; *Special Laws* (1895), chap. 69, chap. 69, articles 8, 9, 10, 11; *R.C.* (1795), articles 1555, 1556; *S.L.* (1899), chap. 161, article 1; *R.C.* (1899), articles 1556, 6156.

26. *Colorado C.L.* (1885), article 3, 221.

27. *Statutes of Oklahoma* (1893), article 2, 86–89; *Territory of Oklahoma Session Laws of 1903,* chap. 2, 46–51.

28. 158 *American Law Reports* 375.

29. *Shannon v. U.S.,* 160 *Fed.* 870 (9th Cir. 1908).

30. 36 *LFR* 261.13 (1919); 43 *CFR* 161.11 (1) (Supp. 1956); Frank Mockler, "The Open Range: A Vanishing Concept," 13 *Wyoming Law Journal* 138 (1959).

31. 220 *U.S.* 523 (1911); Mockler, "Open Range," 137.

32. 5 *Kansas* 433 (1870); 158 *American Law Reports* 375–76.

33. *Richard v. Sanderson,* 39 *Colorado* 270, 89 *Pacific* 769 (1907); *Martin v. Platt Valley Sheep Co.,* 12 *Wyoming* 432, 76 *Pacific* 571 (1904).

34. *Moore v. Pierson,* 93 *S.W.* 1997 (1906), 100 *Texas* 113, 94 *S.W.* 1132 (1906); *Invest & Agency Co. v. McCleland Bros.,* 89 *Texas* 483, 35 *S.W.* 474 (1896).

35. 152 *U.S.* 81.

36. *Haskins v. Andrews,* 12 *Wyoming* 485, 76 *Pacific* 588 (1904).

37. 158 *American Law Reports* 383–84; 12 *Idaho* 148, 85 *Pacific* 384 (1906).

38. 33 *Utah* 362, 93 *Pacific* 994 (1908); 158 *American Law Reports* 384.

39. 83 *S.W.* 726 (1904); 14 *Wyoming* 503, 85 *Pacific* 382 (1906); 158 *American Law Reports* 389.

40. 35 *Colorado* 138, 83 *Pacific* 639 (1905); 158 *American Law Reports* 389.

41. *Paschal's Digest,* article 3840, 640; *General Laws of Texas* (1874), 152; 6 *Texas* 133–36 (1851); 20 *Texas* 816–17 (1859).

42. Casad, "Kansas Law," 58.

43. *Kansas G.S.* (1949), 29–192; Casad, "Kansas Law," 60.

44. Casad, "Kansas Law," 61; Note, 34 *Iowa Law Review* 318, 319 (1949).

45. Alvin Peters, "Herd Laws in Kansas," 20 *Heritage of the Great Plains* (1987), 29.

46. *Laws of Nebraska Territory* (1862), 113–14, 128; (1864), 240, 242–45; (1865), 125; (1866), 734–35; Rodney Davis, "Before Barbed Wire: Herd Law Agitations in Early Kansas and Nebraska," in *Essays in American History in Honor of James C. Malin,* Burton Williams, ed. (1973), 126.

47. *Kansas G.S.* (1949), 47/101–103; Casad, "Kansas Law," 62.

48. *Lauer v. Livings,* 24 *Kansas* 200 (1880).

49. The Kansas territorial legislature, for example, defined such materials as "posts and rails," "posts and palings," "posts and planks," "palisades," "turf," "hedges," "rails," "stone," and "wire." The Nebraska legislature in 1857 sanctioned the diversity of fencing: "Any structure or hedge or ditch, in the nature of a fence, used for purposes of enclosure, which is such as good husbandmen generally keep, and shall, on testimony of skilful men, appear to be sufficient." *Statutes of the State of Kansas* (1855), 416; (1862), 600–601; (1866), 486–87; *Laws of Nebraska,* I:370; Alvin Peters, "Posts and Palings, Posts and Planks," 12 *Kansas History* (1989), 223.

50. Peters, "Posts," 33.

51. *Laws of Kansas* (1872), 384–85; Dykstra, *Cattle Towns,* 39–40.

52. Dykstra, *Cattle Towns,* 31, 297.

53. *Session Laws of Nebraska* (1871), 120–22; Leslie Hewes, "Early Fencing on the Western Margin of the Prairie," 63 *Nebraska History* (1982), 300–48.

54. 7 *Kansas* 364–69; Peters, "Posts," 30; Davis, "Barbed Wire," 129.

55. *Session Laws of Kansas* (1970), 236–38; (1871), 206–208; 208–11; (1872), 384–85; Davis, "Barbed Wire," 130; Peters, "Posts," 222.

56. *Session Laws of 1874,* 203–204; *St. Louis & San Francisco Railway Co. v. Mossman,* 30 *Kansas* 336, 2 Pacific 146 (1883); *Kansas G.S.* (1949), 47/301–308; Casad, "Kansas Law," 62; Peters, "Posts," 31. See also *Session Laws of 1879,* 343–45.

57. *General Statutes of 1889,* chap. 6725; *General Statutes of 1929,* 47/301–47/313; Peters, Posts," 32.

58. *General Statutes* 1011, chap. 105, article 7; 9 *Kansas* 406–408 (1872).

59. 31 *Kansas* 622–34; Peters, "Posts," 35.

60. 21 *Kansas* 449–52; 24 *Kansas* 361–65.

61. 21 *Kansas* 613–22; 37 *Kansas* 445–53; 41 *Kansas* 756–58, 45 *Kansas* 520–22; Peters, "Posts," 223.

62. Gammel, *Laws of Texas,* VIII:1131; Webb, *Great Plains,* 284; *General Laws of Texas* (1874), 152; (1879), 107; (1901), 290–91.

63. *Statutes of Oklahoma* (1893), 86–91.

64. *Territory of Oklahoma Session Laws of 1903,* 46–47.

65. Casad, "Kansas Law," 63.

66. King, "Closing," 53–70.

67. Webb, *Great Plains,* 230–318.

68. Davis, "Barbed Wire," 134–35; Hewes, "Fencing," 340.

69. Edward Dale, *The Range Cattle Industry* (1930), 145–55; Dykstra, "Cattle Towns," 342–43.

70. Webb, *Great Plains,* 286–88; *Wyoming Comp. Statutes,* article 66–501 (Supp. 1957); Mockler, "Open Range," 137.

71. *General Laws of Texas* (1884), 37, 68–71.

72. Webb, *Great Plains,* 315–16.

73. *General Laws of Texas* (1879–84), 34; Webb, *Great Plains,* 316. See also Hayter (1968), "Livestock-Fencing," 121–22.

74. 4 *Colorado App.* 201, 35 *Pacific* 283 (1894); 158 *American Law Reports* 388.

75. 6 *Colorado App.* 186, 40 *Pacific* 156 (1895); 158 *American Law Reports* 388.

76. *Statutes of Oklahoma* (1893), 517.

77. 167 *U.S.* 528, 524–25 (1897).

78. 23 *Statutes* 321, chap. 149 (1885).

79. *U.S. v. Brighton Ranch Co.,* 25 *Fed.* 465 (1885); Michael Finn, "Storm over Red Rim: Private Rights Collide with the Unlawful Inclosures Act," 21 *Land and Water Law Review* (1986), 59.

80. 133 *U.S.* 320, 322 (1890); Finn, "Storm," 59–60.

81. 167 *U.S.* 518, 525–26, 528 (1897).

82. 43 *U.S.C.A.,* articles 315–315r (West 1946 and Supp. 1985); Finn, "Storm," 59.

CALVIN WOODARD

Is the United States a Common Law Country?

GIVEN THE PRESENT unsettled state of affairs in eastern Europe and the Far East, jurisprudence and legal history have gained a rare, unexpected relevance to current events. In many parts of the world the possibility of fundamental legal change exists in more realistic terms than at any time in living memory—indeed, some say, at any time since the French and American revolutions of the late eighteenth century, which (as Marx noted) set off the astonishing series of social revolutions culminating in drives for universal suffrage and the abolition of serfdom, slavery, and the more egregious forms of religious persecution. As reform-minded lawmakers of eastern Europe and elsewhere have an unparalleled opportunity to build new legal systems, so we, in this country, also have a chance to help them shape new legal systems that will, in the next few years, emerge as organic parts of the world infrastructure.

These fortuitous circumstances raise a delicate jurisprudential question: In light of our own experience, what exactly are the legal values that we should most wish to share with other nations and peoples? To many persons, including myself, our most valuable endowment is our common law heritage. That tradition, together with its distinctive attributes, differentiates our law from that of the other major legal systems of the world, such as those based on civil law or Islamic law or socialist law (of the former Soviet Union and its satellite nations.) There is no doubt, however, that the legal systems in both Britain and in this country have undergone such deep changes since 1800 that it is very difficult to say what that tradition is, or even what its most distinctive and important attributes are. I therefore believe we owe it to ourselves, as well as to other nations that may wish to follow our lead, to try to extract from our experience those characteristics we can legitimately attribute to the common law.

As this paper was prepared for the 1992 Walter Prescott Webb Lecture Series, the general theme of which was "English Law and the American Experience," I shall focus my remarks largely on circumstances shaping the "common law," as both a form of law and a legal system, as the term was understood at the end of the eighteenth century—the period following the American revolution (during which the English common law came to be adopted in the United States), on the brink of the "great transformation" that would, in the course of the nineteenth century, catapult the Anglo-American world into modernity.

Any fruitful discussion of "common law" must begin with some agreement as to its meaning. For that purpose, I shall rely upon the usage of two celebrated authorities on the subject, one English and one American: Sir William Blackstone (1723–80) and chancellor James Kent of New York (1763–1847). Writing in the mid-eighteenth century, Blackstone divided English law into two basic categories: the *lex scripta,* or written (statutory) law, and the *lex non scripta,* or unwritten law. The latter (and far more important) law, consisted of "custom," general and local. The common law, he said, was "the General Custom of the Realm."[1]

Chancellor James Kent, the "American Blackstone," spoke of common law in his famous *Commentaries on American Law,* published between 1826 and 1837, as "those principles, usages and rules of action . . . which do not rest for their authority upon any express and positive declaration of the will of the legislature."[2] Kent's definition raises the age-old question: If the authority of the common law does not rest upon that of the legislature, then upon what authority does it rest?

Of course Blackstone had, by suggesting that the authority of the common law is ancient "custom," deepened, rather than clarified, the mystery.[3] For what is custom? Does it exist "out there (or "back there") in some discoverable, albeit unwritten, form? If so, as what? As taboos? As religious convictions? As moral values? As public opinion? Or is it to be measured by some "objective" standard, such as, for example, the judgment of an "impartial spectator" (so admired by Scottish Enlightenment philosophers) or the conduct of a "reasonable and prudent man" (the favorite standard of Anglo-American lawyers)?

The concept of "unwritten law" has long puzzled everyone not trained in the common law legal tradition. No doubt the main reason for confusion is that most persons readily assume that "law" means an order issued directly or indirectly by some authoritative lawgiver, usually in the "thou shall/shalt not" form. "In the beginning," there was what? God? Logos? Law? Whichever came first, it was quickly reduced to writing, for mortals have always found more comfort in the written than the unwritten word.[4] Imagine Judeo-Christian religion without the Gospels, or Roman Law without the Code of Justinian, or, for that matter, Shakespeare without "Hamlet" and his other written works. Thus the age-old struggles between the "letter" and the "spirit" of the authoritative "word."

No word, no canon; no canon, no law. Yet the common law has remained unwritten for some eight hundred years—and, along the way, it has spawned a legal system that is surely one of the two or three strongest in the modern world. How is that possible? To understand our law we must answer that question. To that end, I shall give an account of the circumstances by which this counter-intuitive phenomenon—a legal system based on unwritten law—came into being and flourished over many centuries.

FROM AMORPHOUS CUSTOM TO (UNWRITTEN) COMMON LAW: THE ORAL TRADITION

What we know as the common law system came into being because the early English kings, anxious to win support of their Anglo-Saxon subjects, acknowledged their deference to the authority of "ancient custom." But how was that ancient custom to be known and put to practical use? And in what form was it to be employed?

Still in the dawn of English legal history, the would-be lawyers formed themselves into medieval guilds, subsequently known as the Inns of Court, located in London near the king and his court. Like other chartered guilds and liveried companies of the times, the Inns of Court were granted certain royally sanctioned privileges. They were permitted to select their own members; to determine the terms and conditions of apprenticeship for a career at the bar; to establish the ranks, privileges, and seniority of their members; and to monitor the conduct and performance of their guild members.

By the fourteenth century the four major Inns of Court (Lincoln's Inn, Gray's Inn, the Inner Temple, and the Middle Temple) in London exercised virtual dominion over the three royal courts, the Court of Common Pleas, the King's Bench, and the Court of the Exchequer (later known as the "common law courts").[5] They controlled the courts through their control over the persons who actually "ran" the common law courts: no person could be "called" to the bar (and hence practice in those courts) who was not a qualified member of one of the four Inns; and only those persons "called to the bar" who had attained the uppermost rank of the profession (serjeants-at-law) were, by convention, named to the common law bench.

Thus for many centuries, the procedures and practices of the common law courts were more or less exclusively controlled by a small coterie of persons who shared the peculiar training, rituals, and closed fellowship of the four Inns of Court. Over generations, the relationship between the common law courts and the members of the Inns of Court grew into a complex, symbiotic one: the conventions and practices of the one were reinforced and replicated by the other.

Judges sitting in countless ad hoc cases expressed, orally, their (judicial) opinions on a vast array of exquisitely precise issues growing out of the practical problems bedeviling ordinary citizens/clients. The members of the Inns of Court, young and old, scrutinized those opinions with great care. In time, certain (but not all) opinions of the judges became so familiar to the members of the Inns that they, like coin of the realm, carried their own authority. Known to bench and bar alike, such "cases" came to be regarded as the best available "evidence" of the ancient custom itself. Like acorns they grew, over time, into the mighty oaks later generations came to know as "ancient common law principles." But (and this is the point) those common law principles did not exist in that "custom" shared by everyone in a given society. (As, for example, the custom in this country that men do not wear hats in church but women do.)

The principles of the common law were, rather, of a different order: they were "lawyers' law," knowable only to members of the Inns of Court. The "lawyers' law" was knowable only to lawyers because it existed only in long chains of orally delivered judicial opinions. While prior to the modern era (and the printing press), some volumes of "law reports" did exist in written form, they were collected mainly for lawyers' own private use (e.g., Plowden's Reports) or for circulation among the members of the Inns of Court (e.g., the Year Books). In any event, most cases were not reported at all; many that were, were unreliably reported; and even where well reported, the legal significance of cases might not be apparent to a lay reader. Consider, for example, the comment of Lord Campbell regarding Lord Harcourt, an eighteenth-century chancellor, who made the mistake of offending Vernon, a well-known law reporter. According to Campbell, Vernon, who practiced as a counsel regularly before the chancellor, got even with him by "spitefully suppress[ing] his best decisions, and giv[ing] doubtful ones."[6]

Understanding the legal significance of cases was an integral part of the oral tradition that perpetuated the common law. But it could only be learned in the Inns of Court—by sharing in the work done in chambers and being privy to the informal banter and discourse of the dining halls. Thus for generations, the English common law, though based on general custom, was "lawyers' law" knowable only to the members of the four Inns of Court.

CRACKS IN THE MONOPOLISTIC POWERS OF THE INNS OF COURT: CRITICS OF THE ORAL TRADITION IN THE COMMON LAW

The close, symbiotic relationship between the Inns of Court and the common law courts had grown naturally out of the medieval guild relationship. But for reasons too subtle to detail here, that fit had begun to wear thin. By the eighteenth century, many of the traditional guild functions of the Inns had been lost, though the Inns of Court retained most of their medieval guild powers and privileges. Thus their members who had been "called" to the bar, still enjoyed the sole right to appear in the common law courts (thereby excluding all other lawyers, such as attorneys, solicitors, conveyancers, canonists, and civilians—lawyers trained in the civil law, including admiralty), along with control of legal education, a responsibility increasingly neglected for the past century or so.

Thus in England of the late eighteenth century, the stage was set for the next great development in the history of the common law: a movement to reexamine the common law, as a legal system, independent of its guild associations. Various movements arose to protest the monopolistic grip the Inns of Court held on the common law. A spate of legal texts, such as Blackstone's *Commentaries* (originally delivered as lectures to Oxford undergraduates who had no intention of becoming members of the bar) appeared, all of which sought to reveal to the outside world the mysteries of "lawyers' law." Also of course it was at this time that Jeremy Bentham challenged the entire system, its moral value, its logical basis, its form, and the consequences it produced. By the time of the American Revolution, there were many straws in the wind in England itself portending a sharp reaction against the traditional form of the common law.

THE COMMON LAW JUDICIARY IN ENGLAND

Any criticism of the common law system naturally raised questions about the role of the judiciary. The judges, and only the judges, had the authority to give definitive form to the unwritten law (though as we have seen, they did so with great assistance from their fellow members of the Inns of Court). It is therefore not surprising that—during the eighteenth century, when the "lawyers' law" of the common law system was coming under increased attack—"Judge and Company" (to use Bentham's phrase) likewise became the target of intense criticism.

We shall return to that point below. For the moment, however, we would do well to remember that, in the context of the eighteenth century, it was the "independence" of the English judiciary—not that of the code-based judiciaries of western Europe—that won the admiration of many legal and political commentators. (Montesquieu based his concept of "separation of powers" on the English experience. It is possible that the framers of the American Constitution attributed the idea of "separation of powers" to Montesquieu, rather than to the English reality, because the former, as a Frenchman, was less controversial than the latter.)

Nor should we forget that the "judicial independence" so long associated with the common law played a major role in English political as well as legal history. It actually grew up in the crack of the authority of the English king, noted earlier. That crack was the early royal commitment to the ancient custom, which, as we have seen, became (in the hands of the Inns of Court and judges) the "lawyers' law" version of the common law.

The existence of the "lawyers' law" version of the ancient custom put many otherwise conservative members of the legal profession, bench and bar, under two sovereigns. Though certainly not immune to the influences, subtle and otherwise, of royal power, the common law judges differed from ordinary courtiers and royal appointees in that their status, and high rank (as serjeants) stemmed from their membership and standing in the Inns of Court, not from royal patronage. Thus in the troubled seventeenth century, the demands of strong-willed kings (such as Charles I) forced judges and barristers to choose between obeying their monarch and following the "common law." Bolstered by their Inns of Court training and relationships, some (including Sir Edward Coke) dared follow the common law rather than submit to the "unlawful" will of an unpopular king.

Thus England rejected monarchical absolutism in the seventeenth century—Charles I was beheaded in 1649—a full century before the American and French revolutions. The common law was a significant factor in making it do so. It is not therefore unreasonable to assume that the subsequent rise of anti-authoritarian attitudes in western political thought was, to some extent, influenced by the example of the conscience-splitting choice the members of the English legal profession, bench and bar, faced when their king refused to follow their (unwritten) law. Some of them chose what became our legal tradition.

So much for the English common law at the end of the eighteenth century and the peculiar legal system it engendered. The history of both English and the U.S. law since about 1800 has been a steady retreat from the common law system described above. To turn to the United States in the early national era, we can see that there are good reasons for doubting that the United States was ever a common law country. Those reasons are: (1) our law and legal system is based on our own (written) Constitution, not English custom; (2) throughout most of the nineteenth century, we had no legal institution comparable to, or capable of fulfilling the very essential functions of, the Inns of Court; and (3) American judges have the authority to declare legislation unconstitutional, while their British counterparts have no such power.

THE FORM OF U.S. LAW: THE COMMON LAW IN THE AGE OF CONSTITUTIONS

In the last quarter of the eighteenth century, when the United States was coming into existence, American attitudes toward the common law were divided. Some Americans insisted that the common law was part of their indefeasible heritage and the revolution had been fought in defense of their custom-cum-common law "rights as Englishmen" unlawfully denied them by the tyranny of George III, the usurpations of the privy council, and the corrupt complicity of Parliament.

In fact early American advocates of the common law included many persons who did not associate the common law with England at all, but who regarded it as a form of universal natural law. Consider, for example, the following grandiloquent definition of the "common law" appearing in one of the earliest volumes of American law reports published in this country:

> Common law is the perfection of reason, arising from the nature of God, of man, and of things, and from the relations, dependencies, and connections: It is universal and extends to all men, in every possible situation; and embraces all cases and questions that can possibly arise; it is in itself perfect, clear, and certain; it is immutable, and cannot be changed or altered, without altering the nature and relation of things; it is superior to all other laws and regulations, by it they are corrected and controlled; all positive laws are to be construed by it, and wherein they are opposed to it, they are void.[7]

Other Americans, however, were prepared to wash their hands of England and everything English. Their attitude takes us back to the origins of a nation hatched from a cannonball. Many colonists who had feared that they would be hanged for treason if their revolt failed, were reluctant to turn to English law as the guarantor of their hard won, still fragile independence. Thus shortly after the revolution, the founding fathers broke new ground by adopting a written Constitution. Whether, by ratifying the Constitution, the Americans of that time meant to reject, or to affirm a continuing commitment to the English common law system is, and must remain, an open question.

We can, however, say this much. The Constitution itself is not so much a legal code as it is a blueprint for a government designed to act through "law." While it says little about the content of federal law, and still less about that of the several states, it (like the common law system of England) prescribes a *process*—the process by which the federal government shall make, execute, and implement that law. (The First Amendment is jurisprudentially different from the text. The text is largely concerned with the distribution of governmental powers among the three named branches of government. The Bill of Rights, however, is generally concerned with defining the relationship between the federal government and its subjects.)

Our Constitution, being based on the "separation of powers" doctrine, vested the law-making powers of the federal government exclusively in the Congress. Now recall Chancellor Kent's words: the common law is law that does "not rest for authority upon any express and positive declaration of the will of the legislature." Does our Constitution recognize any law other than that enacted by the Congress?

The status of the common law under our Constitution is at best ambiguous. in the 1840s Justice Joseph Story tangled with the issue in the great case of *Swift v. Tyson.* He held that the Constitution did recognize the existence of federal common law based on some authority other than that of congress. (That case actually involved the Lex Mercatori, the "law merchant" recognized by all the commercial nations of western Europe.) But the issue continued to torment lawyers and judges for almost a century. In the 1930s the Supreme Court overruled Story in *Erie Railroad v. Tompkins,* the court specifically holding that there is no "federal common law."[8]

Fear of the vagaries of the common law was also evident among the state governments. Thus each of the original thirteen states had enacted its own constitution, some of which antedated the U.S. Constitution itself, and the several states admitted to the union after 1792 adopted their own (written) constitutions as well. The law in some states, in which large numbers of the population had emigrated from homelands with no common law tradition, reflected their distinctive heritage. Thus Roscoe Pound, a distinguished legal scholar and dean of the Harvard law school, who was a native of Nebraska, always claimed he grew up in a civil law country because his home state had a code.

The most oft-mentioned models among advocates of codification were the codes of Justinian, Napoleon, Jeremy Bentham, or the more homegrown versions of Edward Livingston and, later, David Dudley Field. In the western territories a number of codes, such as the Kearny Code in New Mexico and the Howell Code in Arizona, were duly adopted before statehood. Though Louisiana was the only state to become officially a civil law state, American dissatisfaction with the (unwritten) common law was widespread, most especially in the area of criminal law. A powerful consensus deplored "common law crime" and by mid-century most states had reduced criminal law to statutory or code form.

THE ABSENCE OF A LEGAL INSTITUTION COMPARABLE TO THE INNS OF COURT

As suggested earlier, the English Inns of Court served a vital function by controlling the professional behavior of their members. In this country, however, we had no Inns of Court to hold lawyers and judges in line. Indeed we scarcely had any legal tradition at all, for law books were scarce and almost no formalized legal education was available. By dint of circumstance, our law was based on a less tutored form of "custom" than that of the English common law. In fact for most of the nineteenth century, except in a few, mainly east coast cities, the standards for membership in the bar were low, and the state of legal education was at best indifferent. Under such circumstances, a legal system based on unwritten common law was highly vulnerable to abuse from all sides.

But not having a bench and bar closely monitored by an American replica of the Inns of Court was not all bad. We are told that ignorance of the nuances of the English common law saved many American lawyers and judges of the nineteenth century from slavish deference to English practices. As Lincoln' friend Justice Miller noted, many American judges "did not know enough [such law] to do the wrong thing so they did the right thing."[9]

For reasons already discussed, English judges enjoyed a striking degree of "judicial independence." Indeed, with the possible exception of Roman law during the republic, the common law may well have been the first major legal system to operate substantially free of personal intervention by the head of state or the more overt forms of political influence. How did American judges compare?

Though our Constitution speaks of the "judicial power" being vested in a supreme court, the nature of that power is not explained. The framers seemed to have assumed, in keeping with the "separation of powers" doctrine, that the role of the judiciary was limited to what Aristotle called "corrective justice:" imposing punishment and resolving disputes arising under laws enacted by congress and applied by the executive branch. Nothing in our Constitution suggests that American judges, state or federal, were to be Blackstonelike "oracles" or "repositories" of American law.

But early in the nineteenth century, Chief Justice John Marshall laid the foundation for a new judiciary. Over the next century and a half, the American judiciary would develop attributes that were, in 1800, quite unimaginable, and indeed inconceivable in any judiciary except (paradoxically) that of the English common law. By the end of the twentieth century, the justices of the United States supreme court came to resemble Blackstone's common law judges, as the oracles of our law.

In his celebrated opinion in *Marbury v. Madison*, Marshall not only invented "constitutional law"—a curious mixture of what Roman lawyers called "private" and "public" law.[10] Having judicially determined that the U.S. Constitution was a legal (as opposed to political) document, he concluded that it, like a statute, could be construed or interpreted *only* by a court of law—namely, the U.S. Supreme Court.

Thus was born the new field of "constitutional law." But he did more. By claiming for the Supreme Court the exclusive right to interpret the Constitution, Marshall implicitly invested American judges with the power to nullify legislation they adjudged to be "unconstitutional"—a power no English court would claim after the Glorious Revolution of 1688, when the principle of "parliamentary sovereignty" was firmly established.

It should be noted that in England, the judges who had rarely exercised the power of striking down legislation, did not exercise that power at all after the revolution of 1688. At that time William and Mary were invited by the Parliament to occupy the throne abandoned by James II. The royal couple agreed to reign, on conditions laid down by Parliament. Thereafter—down to the last few years in fact—it was generally assumed that sovereignty in England was vested in the "king-in-parliament" and hence all statutes enacted by the sovereign were constitutionally binding on judges as well as everyone else. Thus the role of the English judiciary was subordinated to Parliament. As a result, the significance of the ancient custom-cum-common law remains unclear.

What would happen, for example, if Parliament enacted a statute that clashed with the ancient custom—the "Ancient Constitution" or the common law? Who but the judges can say? During the last decade or so, however, there have been insistent demands for an English "bill of rights" that would enumerate in writing the rights of individuals, and would impose upon the courts the responsibility of protecting those individual rights from infringement by parliament or anyone else.

The doctrine of "judicial supremacy" may well be the most original and significant contribution to political and legal theory of the United States. Is it the rejection or the fulfillment of the common law tradition? Looking back on the nineteenth century, we can see that Britain and the United States were struggling with problems arising out of the common law system. In dealing with those problems, they either embraced new legal systems (such as our constitutional-federalism), or they adopted such deep reforms of the common law that both nations ended up with legal systems that neither Blackstone nor Kent could possibly recognize.

The nineteenth-century criticisms of the common law in both Britain and the United States reflected a widespread belief that the traditional legal system was grotesquely out of step with the times. (To many observers, including Charles Dickens, the English legal system consisted of quaint rituals performed by an outlandishly berobed and bewigged class of semipriestly jurists.) As such, it failed totally to respond to rising demands for a more rationalistic, scientific, and egalitarian form of law.

Of course such demands mirrored deeper and wider changes at work in the two nations. The history of both diverged sharply during the nineteenth century. England expanded, literally around the globe, into the world's most powerful empire. At the same time the United States spread ever further west, in fulfilling its own "manifest destiny." A natural result of these developments was that the law of each nation became progressively less like that of the other, and the law of both became less like that of their (common) past.

As England had been, in the seventeenth century, the first nation to free itself from the absolutism of monarchy, so a century later it was the first nation to become industrialized. In the nineteenth century it became the "workshop of the world." Industrialists of the nineteenth century deplored the common law system with its built-in biases in favor of the landed classes. They called for a new form of law that would promote certainty and limited liability. As industrialization progressed, the leaders of the bench and bar responded to the entrepreneurs' complaints. In the last half of the century, the English judiciary and legal system were reorganized.

In 1871–73, Parliament reorganized the entire English court system under a new, single supreme court of judicature. Earlier, the oral tradition of the common law, to which only the members of the Inns of Court had been privy, was substantially replaced by what can only be called a form of "judicial positivism:" the opinions of the common law courts were to be collected, edited, head-noted, and officially published—making them more generally available in a more comprehensible and usable form. At roughly the same time, the judges (who were already obligated by the doctrine of "parliamentary sovereignty" to defer strictly to the enacted law) bound themselves to follow their own earlier rulings: they thereby cast the long-standing practice of following persuasive precedent into an ironclad rule of *stare decisis* (whereby all earlier cases on the same point must be followed). Thus the scope of the unwritten common law was narrowed by statute, and the discretion of Blackstone's oracles was substantially curtailed. The customary role of the common law had been drastically changed.

While the new industrial entrepreneurs were clamoring for a more rational and efficient legal system to replace the outmoded common law, the "lower" classes were demanding more legal protection and assistance. Having been drawn to the cities, mill towns, and factories from farms, and inexperienced in urban living, such persons made up a new social class, what E. P. Thompson called England's new "working class." Exposed to hideous living conditions and peculiarly vulnerable to exploitation, they joined together for protection and protest. As the common law courts had traditionally been closed to them and their concerns (except when they were accused of crime), they pinned their hopes on politics and legislation enacted by a reformed and slightly more sympathetic parliament. (Disraeli once observed that the history of the nineteenth century was neatly summarized by a single change in the language of the law: the shift from "master/servant"—the traditional social relationship, recognized by common law, redolent of a world of manor houses and landed estates—to "employer/employee," an entirely new legal relationship created by a statute recognizing trade unions.)

Ironically, for much of the nineteenth century the common law was seen in England by employers to be too uncertain to meet their economic needs, and by employers to be too narrow and legalistic to respond adequately to their needs. Satisfying neither, the common law became a target for both.

Consequently, at the beginning of the twentieth century the future of the common law in England was, at best, uncertain. For by then, the Fabian Society and the newly legalized trade unions had captured a wide following among the newly enfranchised classes. They put their hopes for social reform not in the common law but in "administrative law," an alien form of law borrowed from the continent, which (as A. V. Dicey asserted at the time) was profoundly incompatible with the common law. The English welfare state of the twentieth century consists of agencies created or recognized by administrative law. As a consequence, the role and prestige of the English judiciary has declined.

So much for the English efforts to accommodate to, and to preserve, the common law tradition. As already noted, starting with the framing of our Constitution, the relationship in the United States with the common law has been streaked with this same ambivalence. We now add that, from the end of the Civil War down to the First World War, American law was increasingly influenced not by English, but continental, legal scholars (who were trained in the civil law tradition). Thus the idea of "sociological jurisprudence," and the jurisprudence of "interests," "administrative law," "criminology," and, later, "legal realism"—and indeed "jurisprudence" itself—all found their way into American legal thought, which was, increasingly, becoming less practitioner-dominated. Indeed by 1900, American law had already begun to be a research-oriented profession taught in university-based law schools by law professors (not moonlighting practitioners) who regarded themselves primarily as legal scientists.

That trend has continued in this century. Indeed it may be that at the end of the twentieth century such professors are now the "oracles" of our law. If so, the law they dominate is not the common law. It is, rather, a modern-day policy-oriented science.

For almost two centuries, Anglo-Americans have been busily rejecting the common law. There have been countless attempts to make it into something else: a code or a science, or to construct, on logical foundations, the legal institutions that evolved naturally through the workings of the common law system. Countless legal scholars have made forays beyond the boundaries of the common law process into other fields and sciences, always searching for that extralegal elixir, which, when added to the narrow "lawyers' law" of the common law, will make it real law.

We are, however, still asking ourselves the same questions about the common law that troubled the founders of this nation in 1789. What is the relationship between U.S. law and the English common law? And, as noted at the outset, looking beyond our own backyard, we have to wonder what aspects of our common law tradition we should most want to see emulated and replicated elsewhere. I myself think the greatest single value of the common law tradition is the skeptical attitude it has engendered toward "law." Perhaps this point is best illustrated by a comparison of noncommon law (German) and the U.S. lawyers' attitudes toward certainty in law. Associating the American attitude with Justice Holmes's famous metaphor about the "marketplace of free ideas," one author observed that there is no such skepticism among German lawyers. To them, he said, "there is only one answer under law."[11]

As already stated, the common law actually developed in the crack between the *authority* of law ("ancient custom") and all other *forms* of law, including the king's will. That difference fostered and made creditable the idea that there existed somewhere—out there, up there, or back there—a kind of authority greater than that of the king himself. It also gave rise to a dispassionate attitude toward law that freed subjects of the common law from one of the oldest, and still widest spread forms of human tyranny: the blind, superstitious, often irrational response to everything labeled "law."

NOTES

1. William Blackstone, *Commentaries on the Laws of England* (Oxford: Clarendon Press, 1765).

2. James Kent, *Commentaries on American Law,* William Kent, ed. (4 volumes; 7th edition: New York, 1851).

3. Orthodox common law theory not only assumed that the (unwritten) common law principles were derived from ancient custom. It also held that common law "principles" were both comprehensive and eternal. Thus according to an oft quoted maxim, no "new" case could ever arise at common law, for however novel the facts may be, they were covered by some already existing common law principle. Take, for example, the law regarding the rights of passengers on jet airplanes. In one sense no such problem could possibly have arisen before the twentieth century. To the common law lawyer, however, the matter was covered by a principle of ancient vintage. In earlier times, it had dealt with the duties public ferrymen owed their passengers. Later, that principle was extended to deal with stagecoach operators, and later still, with railroad companies. Thus while jet airplanes are surely modern, the principle governing the rights of passengers is as old as the need for public transportation—and ancient common law addressed it.

4. I cannot resist quoting a remark by a famous Roman Law scholar of the last century: "A close adherence to the letter is a mark of unripeness everywhere, and especially in law. The history of law might write over the first chapter, as a motto, 'In the beginning was the word.' To all rude people the word appears something mysterious, whereas it being written or solemnly uttered as a formular, and their simple faith fill it with supernatural power" (Richard Von Ghering, *Geist des Römischen Rechts,* Band II [1864], Teil 2, 441).

5. The Court of Chancery is sometimes regarded as a "common law court." Because it was never based on "ancient custom," I believe it was totally different in origin and purpose, as well as jurisdiction. Though an influential part of English law, it was not common law. The place of "equity" (as distinguished from "chancery law"—the paralegal system that, in England, grew up around the chancellor and the chancery), is always a major jurisprudential, as well as legal, problem. We in this country are still grappling with it. See Calvin Woodard, "Joseph Story and American Equity," 45 *Washington and Lee Law Review* 623 (1988).

6. Campbell continued: "I suspect that the reporter may have been a Whig, and

copied the Tory blacksmith, who in shoeing the horse of a Whig lamed him. See 2 *Vernon,* 664–688. When I was a *nisi prius* reporter I had a drawer marked 'Bad Law' into which I threw all the cases which seemed to me to be improperly ruled. I was flattered to hear Sir James Mansfield, C.J., say, 'Whoever reads Campbell's reports must be astonished to find how uniformly Lord Ellenborough's decisions were right'" (John Campbell, *The Lives of the Lord Chancellors* [London, 1846], IV, 458).

7. J. Root, *Introduction to Reports of Cases adjudicated in the [Connecticut] Superior Court and Supreme Court of Errors from July 1789 to June 1793* (1798). Note especially Root's view that statutes that clashed with the common law were void. Note also that this view was current before Marshall's famous decision in *Marbury v. Madison,* of 1803, in which he held that statutes that clashed with the federal Constitution were void.

8. *Swift v. Tyson,* 16 *Peters* 1 (1842); *Erie Railroad v. Tomkins,* 304 U.S. 65 (1938).

9. Quoted in R. Pound, *The Formative Era of American Law* (1938), 11.

10. *Marbury v. Madison,* 1 *Cranch* 137 (1803).

11. The author adds: "Whoever does not have or need certainty may have confidence in discussion and criticism but German law is governed by an unbounded nostalgia for a certainty. . . . The science in which the lawyer is trained is not experimental, but hermeneutic; here, the interpretation of texts is far more important than an independent relation to the realities of past and present. Such science engenders attitudes that must be called subordinate, if not servile, rather than polemical; the certainty of the German lawyer is based on unmovable givens, not their own insights" (R. Dahrendorf, *Society and Democracy in Germany* [Anchor Books, 1969], 231). Dahrendorf, who has since moved to England, become master of an Oxford college, and been knighted, first published his comparison (in German) in 1965. I can only hope that his American attitudes toward law continue to be as skeptical of authority as he assumed them to be at that time.